THE ART OF
CREATIVE
THINKING

Other books by Wilferd A. Peterson

The Art of Getting Along
The Art of Living
The New Book of the Art of Living
More About the Art of Living
Adventures in the Art of Living
The Art of Living in the World Today
The Art of Living Day By Day
The Art of Living Treasure Chest

THE ART OF CREATIVE THINKING

WILFERD A. PETERSON

Hay House, Inc.
Santa Monica, CA

THE ART OF CREATIVE THINKING
by Wilferd A. Peterson

Copyright © 1991 by Wilferd A. Peterson

Library of Congress Catalog Card No. 90-71111

Library of Congress Cataloging-in-Publication Data

Peterson, Wilferd Arlan, 1900–
    The art of creative thinking / Wilferd A. Peterson.
        p.   cm.
    Essays originally published in the author's column in
Science of Mind magazine since 1964.
    Includes bibliographical references.
    ISBN 1-56170-004-5 : $10.00
    1. Conduct of life.   I. Title.
BJ1581.2.P485   1991   90-71111
153.3'5—dc20   CIP

ISBN: 1-56170-004-5

Internal design by Teri Stewart
Typesetting by Freedmen's Typesetting Organization,
Los Angeles, CA 90004

91 92 93 94 95 96   10 9 8 7 6 5 4 3 2 1
First Printing, January 1991

Published and Distributed in the United States by:

Hay House, Inc.
501 Santa Monica Boulevard
Post Office Box 2212
Santa Monica, California 90406 USA

Printed in the United States of America on Recycled Paper

Dedicated to my daughter,
Mrs. Lilian Grace Thorpe

TABLE OF CONTENTS

FOREWORD

One evening recently, on a trip to the beach, I stood and gazed out at the ocean. The dance of the moonlight on it gave the appearance of diamonds glittering just under the water's surface, radiant gems simply waiting to be scooped out. That image came to mind as I sat down to write the foreword to this book, *The Art of Creative Thinking*, for I also see in it the presence of sparkling gems—gems of light, inspiration, and truth, waiting for you to mine.

Wilferd Peterson draws upon a rich store of experience, acquired during more than eight decades of creative living. The writing contained here, done over a period of many years, testifies to his unquenchable zest for life, his openness to the wonder and newness of it, and his deep appreciation for its great and marvelous gifts.

He will challenge, nurture, delight, and uplift you, as you explore creativity with him, finding along the way an astonishingly vast territory of possibility you may never have dreamed existed.

Whether he is talking about serendipidity, gratitude, work, surprise, fantasy, or heroes, Bill Peterson offers a fresh perspective on a wide-ranging variety of life's aspects. He makes us look at everything just a little bit differently. And then we are changed.

For me, that is the joy of reading his essays. They open my mind and heart to a fuller realization of all that is potential within me—as well as within all of us. They awaken in me a greater sense of aliveness. Yes, Bill has a special flare for leading his readers gently, eloquently, to the deep well within.

He imparts the message, not only through his writings but also through his own life experience, that to think creatively is to be fully, exuberantly, expressively alive. He rivets our attention to the truth that to be creative is to be drenched with the enthusiasm, energy, and excitement that flow when we have drunk from that deep well, when we have touched what is universal within us all.

So I invite you to join the thousands of readers of *Science of Mind* Magazine, who have for many years been inspired and empowered by his "Creative Adventure" column, to enter fully into the exciting quest to which Bill beckons us. Discover and expand your own creativity. Dive into the treasure chest of your own inner richness.

Sparkling gems of wisdom, truth and inspiration lie spread here before you to point the way!

—Kathy Juline
Editor, *Science of Mind* Magazine

PREFACE

To me, creativity has always been a hobby, but it has grown beyond that to become a philosophy and a way of life.

First it is about *creating things*; new, different, better things, or improvements on old, established things. It is about abundant living for everyone. It is about better homes, schools, colleges and places to work. It is about creating peace and good will among people everywhere.

Next, it is important to *create ourselves*. To make the most of our physical, mental and spiritual potential. And then to live a *creative life* and pass creativity around to those who cross our path.

With these creative ideals in mind that is what this book is all about. Creativity has been my joy. First, I've worked at it as a human being attempting to put creative principles to work in my own life, with personal growth as my goal. Then, I have endeavored to spread creativity around, as salesman, business executive, advertising man, and author of eight book on the *Art of Living*. It was natural that when I began, in 1964, to write a monthly page for *Science of Mind* magazine, I entitled it, *The Creative Adventure*.

And now the best of these essays have been collected in a book, it has taken a quarter of a century to write. Here is all I know, *so far*, about how to be a Creative Thinker . . .

ACKNOWLEDGEMENTS

My first article to appear in *Science of Mind* magazine was in the January 1964 issue. It was entitled, "Happy New You" and appears in this book as "Creative Happiness." It was the beginning of more than a quarter of a century of writing on the subject of creativity. This book is a response to many requests to have the best of my writings on creativity available in a single volume. I thank the editors of *Science of Mind* for making this book a reality.

All references to personalities, as well as quotations from them, appear as part of the text. I am grateful for this inspiration which has been in many ways the heart of this book.

My thanks, also, to my editor, Dan Olmos of Hay House, to my associate, Cathie Bloom, who has contributed many ideas and suggestions during the preparation of the manuscript, and to the many readers of *Science of Mind*, who have asked for this volume.

May it help you to master the art of creative thinking.

INTRODUCTION

Today we possess the greatest legacy of genius and creativity ever known.

The creative adventure began at least ten thousand years before the birth of Jesus, with prehistoric man's first crude drawings on the walls of caves. Through these images, he began to communicate the ideas in his mind. The discovery of fire, the invention of the wheel, the boat, and the sail, began a whole stream of revolutionary discoveries and inventions that have fashioned the world we live in today. Our idea of a creative force in the universe has evolved, too, from the primitive God of fear, terror, and vengeance . . . to a God of love.

With this rich legacy of the past, we face today with a limitless creative potential.

The world around us is a stimulus for us to make our creative contribution. Every library is a treasure house of the genius of the ages. There we can live and work with the greatest scientists, writers, inventors, artists, architects, and other men and women of achievement. We can be companions of Leonardo da Vinci, William Shakespeare, Elizabeth Barrett Browning, Rembrandt, Georgia O'Keefe, Thomas Jefferson, Abraham Lincoln, Golda Meir, and thousands of others who will inspire our own creative spirits. Their successes will stimulate our efforts, their failures will help us avoid the pitfalls of the past. No other source in the world has so much to offer in the living of a great life.

We can travel the world, too, and follow the paths of those who made everlasting marks on every phase of the history of man's life.

"If I have seen farther than others," wrote Isaac Newton, *"it is because I have stood on the shoulders of giants."*

Today, each of us can stand on the shoulders of the greatest men and women who have ever lived. This is our legacy of creativity. No man or woman of the past has had the creative opportunity we have today.

FOUR STEPS TO CREATIVITY

The Creative Process

The following four step gives the most condensed, complete and simple explanation I have discovered about how the creative mind works. It draws upon the scientific contributions of the German physicist Hermann Von Helmholtz and Graham Wallas of the University of London.

Step Number One

SATURATION

. . . Filling the Mind With Data

The first step in creative thinking has no magic in it. It is hard, grueling, brain-beating work!

The dictionary tells us that the word "*saturate*" means "*to treat, furnish, charge (with something) to the point where no more can be absorbed.*" Thorough, painstaking research is the foundation of creative thinking.

Thomas Edison's approach to a problem is a good example of *Saturation.* He said, "*I am more of a sponge than an inventor.*" When he wanted to discover something, he first read how others had attempted to solve the problem in the past. Then he gathered data from the thousands of experiments others had performed and studied that. This was only his starting point for his own attack on the problems. Perhaps this is why he observed: "*Genius is 99 percent perspiration and only 1 percent inspiration.*"

To remind myself of the vital necessity of breaking through human inertia and starting the thinking process, Edison had a framed motto of Joshua Reynolds hanging above his desk. It read: "*There is no expedient* to which man will not resort to avoid the real labor of thinking." Mental laziness is the arch enemy of creative thinking. Leonardo da Vinci, one of the great creative thinkers of all times, must have realized this fact, too, for he exclaimed, "Oh, God, you sell us everything for the price of an effort."

The price of an idea is intensive, concentrated, conscious thinking. You must combine, adapt, and rearrange! But at the same time that you are working on a problem on the conscious level, you are also saturating your subconscious mind with the elements from which the answer may flash. You've prepared the soil and planted the seed. You have given the subconscious mind the data with which to work. Having pushed your conscious mind to the limit without finding the answer, you can now confidently switch to your subconscious mind and let it take over.

Step Number Two

INCUBATION

. . . *Harnessing the Power of the*
Subconscious Mind

The second step in creative thinking is a passive one. You relax, loaf, let go, walk away from your problem and let it simmer in your subconscious mind. Your subconscious mind is the storehouse of all that you have learned and experienced in your lifetime. In some mysterious way it works while you relax to convert the data you have given it into new concepts and patterns.

Relaxation is the key to the subconscious mind. Helmholtz said that his best ideas came to him *"during the ascent of a wooded hill on a sunny day."* Others have found playing golf, fishing, listening to music, or reading detective stories the best way to let the subconscious work.

Relaxation will often remove mental blocks instantaneously. A scientist who had labored far into the night seeking to solve a problem decided to give up and go to bed. As he switched from consciously thinking about his problem and reached to untie a knot in a shoelace the answer he sought flashed into his mind.

Breaking mental tension by brief moments of relaxation—walking to the drinking fountain, looking out of a window, reading a few pages from a book—will frequently cause a flow of new ideas from your subconscious mind. More and more people in business are depending upon their intuition, which simply means awareness of the power of the subconscious.

For one of my talks, an artist made a little character to represent the subconscious. We called the character "Subby." Slides show the thinker hitting a stone wall, and Subby jumping over it and going on with his work. Or Subby at the typewriter while the thinker slept, to waken with the headlines he needed. Or Subby presenting a list of the ideas needed by the thinker. It proved a dramatic way to impress the power of the subconscious on my audience.

The best time of all to command the subconscious is at bedtime. Go over your problems in your mind one by one. Tell yourself that you will have the answers in the morning, keep your expectations high. Subby always proves a good partner. Put him to work.

When you harness the magic power of your subconscious mind, you extend your creative hours around the clock—24 hours a day—while working and loafing, awake and asleep. You multiply your power of achievement!

Step Number Three
ILLUMINATION

. . . *Watching for the Idea Flashes From Your Mind*

Illumination is the actual flash of creative inspiration that comes from your subconscious mind during a period of incubation.

There are specific ways in which you can stimulate and increase the flashes of *Illumination*. It is good to maintain an attitude of quiet expectancy. The supply of ideas in the universe is inexhaustible. Always keep your mental door open. Believe that the idea you need will come to you. Do not reject ideas too soon or discriminate against them too severely. Remove all barriers of critical judgment. Provide a free channel for the flow of ideas.

Practice being aware, wide awake, keep your eyes and ears open to the slightest intimation of an idea. Walk through stores, crowds, art galleries, and streets. Watch how people live. Seek impressions. Ask yourself questions. Be nosey. Learn from everyone. Read more.

You can also create ideas by loafing and meditating in solitude. Emerson recommended that we spend an hour a day in this way. Such meditation develops deep intuitive insights into problems and projects.

Have a quiet "thinking room," or corner, where you can find release from pressure and have time to think about your life and plans for the future.

Once ideas begin to come, write them down . . . at once! Many good ideas have escaped forever because people trusted their memories. "*The strongest memory is weaker than the palest ink*," says a Chinese proverb. Always carry a notebook, and keep another at your bedside.

Step Number Four

VERIFICATION

. . . *Checking, Evaluating, and Polishing Ideas*

Helmholtz confined his analysis of the steps in creative thinking to the three we have covered . . . *Saturation, Incubation,* and *Illumination.* These three steps actually cover the creative process. The fourth setp—*Verification*—has to do with "proving, confirming, and substantiating" ideas. The fourth step was added by Graham Wallas of the University of London, another pioneer researcher in the techniques of creative thinking.

There is sound wisdom in having *Verification* come at the end of the creative process. To interject judgment and critical analysis would stop the flow of ideas. To think or say, *"It can't be done," "It won't work," "It is impossible,"* would stop ideas in their tracks.

In both personal and group thinking the first objective should be to think up as many ideas as possible . . . *to strive for quantity.* All ideas should be written down—the good ones and the bad ones, the ridiculous ones and the funny ones—as they come without attempting to judge their value. Create a "stockpile" of ideas.

Then comes the final step of *verification*. As you check and evaluate, you'll find the "stockpile" of ideas a gold mine of possibilities. The idea you laughed at may be found, on analysis, to contain a hint for a completely new approach to an important problem. An idea that seemed far-fetched when you first heard it may open the way to the development of a new product. An idea that sounded "crazy" may provide a clue for an advertising theme.

You'll find raw ideas that can be shaped and polished into usefulness; you'll find wild ideas that can be tamed and harnessed to do specific jobs. Some ideas will be discarded, of course, but many will be found of priceless value.

Verification should be done by a committee of experienced creative thinkers who understand the precious value of good ideas.

One of America's greatest industrial organizations has a slogan for its engineers which expresses in one sentence, the dynamic approach to creative thinking: *"Let your imagination soar . . . then engineer it down to earth."*

Creative Adventure

Y*OU* ARE AN adventure.

There is inspiring life within you. You live and move and have your being in the Infinite. Vast resources of energy, talent, skill, and genius flow into your life.

You are a bundle of mysteries. Finding and conquering yourself is a lifetime task. There are unplumbed depths in you full of a rich ore awaiting personal discovery. Explore yourself!

There is a power in you—the power to change yourself and to change the world; the power to create plans, projects, movements for the common good; the power to inspire and serve.

There are miracles within you. Within you are books to write, songs to sing, pictures to paint, sermons to preach, inventions to develop, medicines to discover, bridges and cathedrals to build, truths to reveal . . . out of you great work will come.

You are master of your own life. You will rise to

each difficulty with courage and faith. You will meet the challenge of each moment with imagination and daring.

You embrace in your unconscious mind millions of years of experience and wisdom. You stand at the apex of evolution. You will prove your creativity by reaching for things beyond your grasp, by excelling yourself.

You will meet setbacks with bounce and resiliency. You will go on, for as a Hindu Master has said: *"There is no limit to the developing self that steadily and vigorously wills to unfold."*

Venture yourself! Venture all that you are and all that you may become. Magnify yourself; multiply the ways in which you contribute to life.

Creative Affirmation

AN AFFIRMATION IS MORE than just words that are spoken. An affirmation is a belief, a dedication. It is a powerful statement of personal understanding. The dictionary says that to affirm is "to declare positively or firmly, maintain to be true."

An affirmation is you identifying yourself with the goodness of God. *"I am love." "I am joy." "I am peace."*

Affirmations are holy. They are mountaintop thinking.

When I was a young man I discovered an affirmation for the beginning of my day that changed my life. It was written in Sanskrit, an ancient language of India used for sacred and scholarly writing. It was called "The Salutation of the Dawn."

Each morning I faced the east and affirmed its magic words. Later, when I married and had a child, my wife and daughter joined me in the ceremony. Then, still later I taught it to my grandchildren. And today I have been joined by four great-grandsons who are carrying on the tradition.

No finer, more inspiring way can be found to start one's day than with this Sanskrit classic. I invite you to join me in . . .

The Salutation of the Dawn

Listen to the Salutation of the Dawn!
  *Look to **this** day!*
For it is Life, the very Life of Life.
In its brief course lie all the Varieties
    and Realities of your existence;
  The bliss of Growth,
  The Glory of Action,
  The Splendor of Beauty.
For Yesterday is but a dream,
And tomorrow is only a vision.
  *But **today** well lived makes*
Every yesterday a Dream of Happiness,
And every tomorrow a Vision of Hope.
  *Look well, therefore, to **this** day;*
  Such is the Salutation of the Dawn.

Creative Awareness

Aperson is alive only to the degree that he or she is aware. To make the most of life we must constantly strive to be aware of the importance of being aware.

Be Aware of Yourself: We should be aware of who we are and what we want to be. We should be aware of our ideals and purposes and our relationship to the Infinite.

Be Aware of Your Senses and Use Them: So often we are distracted and unconscious of the riches our senses can pour into our lives. We eat food without tasting it, listen to music without hearing it, smell without experiencing the pungency of odors and the delicacy of perfumes, touch without feeling the grain or texture, and see without appreciating the beauty around us.

Be Aware of People: This calls for sensitivity, an empathy that will make us aware of the inner thoughts of people—sadness, loneliness, discouragement, joy. This is often an extrasensory awareness. We should see people not as part of a crowd, but as individuals with needs, longings, and aspirations.

Be Aware of Our Environment: We should be aware of our surroundings, both our community and our country, and of the influences that now mold our world so that we can play our part in the life of our times. We should be aware of significant events in politics, science, and religion and find in them the true and meaningful.

The secret of being more vitally alive is to be more aware. Starting today, from this moment, become aware of awareness!

Creative Beginning

O NCE, BACK IN MY advertising days, I wrote a book-let entitled *Ideas . . . the Beginning of All Things.* The cover, dramatically illustrated by an artist, showed a huge block of marble. Facing the marble was Michelangelo, his hand grasping a chisel. In the head of Michelangelo was an image of his proposed statue of the shepherd boy, David. The sculptor was shown ready to go to work to make his mental image a reality.

Then as the cover of the booklet was opened, the reader was greeted by a full page illustration of the complete statue.

The first paragraph of text read: *"Michelangelo had an idea! From a huge block of marble he resolved to chisel a mighty statue of David. The mental picture in his mind was the spark, the stimulus, the inspiration for the creative masterpiece he fashioned with his hands."*

In all spheres of life it is the same. Ideas are the beginning of all things. Edison had the idea that he could light the world with electricity and he achieved his goal. Fulton had the idea of that steam could be used to power ships and the idea became a reality. Marconi had the idea that messages could be sent through space without the use of wires, and now we have the miracle of television. Marie Curie believed in the existence of yet-undiscovered elements. In her lab, in an isolated shack, she was finally able to isolate both radium and polonium. Today, modern technology is filling the world with new wonders, all ideas coming alive.

The most dynamic, powerful, revolutionary thing on earth is an idea. Humanity has moved upward on a ladder of ideas from the invention of the wheel to the magical flights of the shuttle.

The world we live in today first existed in the minds of people . . . bridges, skyscrapers, machines, religions, philosophies, governments, musical compositions, poems . . . everything!

Our future is vast because God has given us the unlimited power to create ideas. Each day is a challenge to explore new possibilities, to adventure with new ideas that will make our lives richer and better.

Creative thinkers sculpt the world!

Creative Brainstorming

WHEN BATTEN, BARTON, DURSTINE AND OSBORN, Inc., the New York advertising agency, first be-gan experimenting with "brainstorming", I went there to observe how they used it.

Brainstorming is an exciting process by which in-dividuals strive to stimulate and inspire each other to create ideas. The purpose is to tap the subconscious mind of each member in a group and create a mutual sharing of the mental wealth of all those participating. Through the mechanism of association, one idea will suggest another and another . . . creating a chain reac-tion of many more ideas.

The use of a blackboard, on which the leader writes down the ideas, helps to focus attention on the problem. And setting a goal of a certain number of ideas—perhaps ten or one hundred—creates an idea-target to shoot at, adding zest to the meeting.

The individual participants need to bring to this process a positive spirit of success and enthusiasm.

They must strive to build an atmosphere of relaxation, freedom, and fellowship, with everyone encouraged to take part. Negative attitudes and fear of criticism and ridicule should be completely abolished.

The value of brainstorming is not confined to the advertising business. It can be used by everyone from engineers to writers, and by political conferences, church gatherings, service clubs, or any other group. Brainstorming is thinking-together, harnessing imaginative power. It is mental teamwork, going into a creative-huddle. It can be used by family members to create harmony in the home or by statesmen to create a peaceful world.

Wherever you are, whoever you are, whatever your project, brainstorming will widen the horizons of your thinking.

Creative Browsing

THERE ARE TWO BASIC levels of creative thinking. First, there is the *voluntary level*, where you apply your will, your initiative, and your knowledge to the creation of ideas or the solving of problems. Second, there is the *involuntary level*, where ideas unexpectedly explode into your mind without any conscious effort on your part, while you are simply waiting.

The key to effective creative thinking is to strike a balance between creative working and creative waiting.

I have discovered that browsing is a very effective way to wait creatively. Browsing is leisurely and casual and can be done almost anywhere. You can browse through a museum, an art gallery, a department store, or a library. I've also found old bookstores to be treasure houses of wonderful volumes, fertile ground for creative waiting.

But most of all I like to spend an afternoon in my own study, browsing through my many shelves of books. Here are books collected over more than fifty years. I just reach out spontaneously and pick out a book, any book. Sometimes it is a volume I haven't opened in many years and I discover thoughts that inspired me long ago. Once again these thoughts come alive and lift my spirits.

Sometimes I search specifically for a book I want to reread. I may even fail to find it. But if, in my search, I rediscover a number of volumes I had long forgotten, I am inspired again by words that once shaped my life. Browsing through my books is also a process of renewal. I check the sentences and paragraphs I had long ago underlined with a red pencil. I awaken to old dreams and ideals.

Books are indeed, as someone has called them, "embalmed minds." Writers dead for hundreds of years speak again. The wisdom of the ages is ours to command.

Never neglect the great creative adventure of browsing though your books.

Creative Celebration

IT SEEMS TO ME that once each year we should have a holiday to celebrate how creativity has enriched our lives as individuals.

I consider myself, for example. Born in 1900, at the turn of the century, I have reached the ripe old age of 90. I have had a ringside seat at many of the amazing creative changes that have taken place during my lifetime.

It would take all the pages of this book and more to list the miracles that have happened. As a boy I read many books by the light of a kerosene lamp, then was able to welcome the coming of electricity. I remember my first ride in an automobile, my first flight in an airplane, (at Kitty Hawk I have seen a model of the first plane in which the Wright Brothers flew, and I have also flown the ocean many times in a huge jetliner.)

I took my Saturday bath as a boy in a washtub, then later came to enjoy the luxury of inside plumbing. I experimented with the wireless and welcomed the coming of radio and television. My first automobile was a Model T Ford that had to be started with a crank. (Since then I have driven many different cars and still own one of 1972 vintage.) The invention of the fountain pen was a great event in my life and now I am amazed at what is being done with computers.

I have also been enriched by the creative people I have met—the teachers, preachers, professors, friends, my wife, the children—all who have brought me knowledge and happiness. I am thankful for the thinkers who, with God's help, have created the wonderful world in which I live.

And I must not forget my blessed books, which surround me in my study where I am writing these words on an old Royal typewriter almost as old as I am.

What about the creative thinking of the future? It should be greater than ever. It should multiply and expand. It should be about things but also about thoughts. It should not limit itself to computers but it should also reach out to causes. It should concentrate on abolishing war and creating an enduring peace. It should strive to reduce hunger and poverty. It should be open to expanding the goodness of God on earth.

Creative Children

IN HIS SERMON on the Mount, Jesus said: *"Blessed be the Peace Makers for they shall be called the Children of God."*

To glorify childhood the above words might be paraphrased to say: *"Blessed be Children for they shall be called the Peace Makers of God."* This would make Children the Eternal symbol of Peace.

Later Jesus gathered little children around him and said: *"Suffer the little children to come unto me, and forbid them not, for of such is the Kingdom of Heaven."*

Jesus gave little children Mountain-Top recognition.

When we list the creative qualities of children, we discover that they express creative values that adults might well use in building the peace.

Here are some of those values:
* The playful attitude;
* Believing the unbelievable;
* Imagination;
* Love and forgiveness;
* Curiosity and openness;

16

* Simplicity;
* Faith and trust;
* Good will;
* Joy, fun and laughter;
* Goodness;
* Eagerness and enthusiasm;
* Prayer;
* Loyalty;
* Belief in dreams and myths.

My five-year-old great grandson, who calls me "Great," has this myth about me: *"Great,"* he says, *"is one hundred years old. He is a millionaire and he writes books."*

In our search for peace let us apply the creative wisdom and spirit of children . . . to simplify the complex, to come down to earth to save the earth, to practice the ABC's of human relationships.

Creative Circle

WHEN I STEPPED INTO Ralph Waldo Emerson's study in his home in Concord, Massachusetts, what impressed me most was that he had sat in a Boston rocker and worked at a circular table. Here he wrote in his Journal and penned his immortal essays. Here he wrote the material that makes him today, after one hundred years, still America's most quoted writer.

What mystic spell the circular table must have cast over Emerson! The circle is, in fact, the symbol of so many things he believed in: eternity, God, wholeness, never-ending power, the over-soul, the fact that man himself is a self-evolving, expanding circle of creativity.

Sitting at this very table, Emerson wrote one of his most inspiring essays, "Circles." "St. Augustine," he wrote, "*described the nature of God as a circle whose center was everywhere and its circumference nowhere. Our life is an apprenticeship to the truth that around every circle another can be drawn; that there is no end in nature, but every end is a beginning; that there is always another dawn risen on mid-noon and under every deep a lower deep opens.*"

What a challenge to creativity! To know that our

ability to create is a continuing circle that never ends! Nothing can hold back the creative thinker; his thinking is much like perpetual mental motion, drawing on Infinity. Ideas do not end, but go on and on forever, expanding, evolving, changing, growing.

The mind of the creative thinker never stops. It goes on, as in a circle, exploring every possibility, looking for clues, hints, illuminations. Somewhere in the circle the magic answer awaits.

There are no roadblocks in a circle. There are no stopping points. Around and around the mind goes, around the stars in the sky and the problems of earth . . . searching, exploring, seeking answers.

The next time you are looking for an idea or trying to solve a difficult problem, reach out for the pad on your desk and draw a circle. Let it remind you of the infinite potential of creativity.

Creative Companions

WALK WITH THE dreamers, the believers, the courageous, the cheerful, the planners, the doers, the successful people with their heads in the clouds and their feet on the ground. Walk with those who have ideals, with zest to help and lift, to create and contribute. Let their spirit ignite a fire within you to leave this world better than when you found it.

Shun the doubters, the fearful, the discouraged, the defeated. Shut the door of your mind to their influence.

Associate with the creative people wherever you find them. Make friends with them, go where they are, talk with them, listen to them, be open and receptive to them, let them inspire you. Catch their attitudes, their way of thinking and living.

Some of these people you will find in real life. Others you will find in books. Creative thinkers, many dead for thousands of years, are as alive in their books today as when they walked the earth. Associate with creative minds in poetry, philosophy, psychology, and the masterpieces of fiction. Let them be your companions, help you think creative thoughts. Read the stories of creative achievers in biography and autobiography; men and women who left their mark through their immortal creative contributions to life.

Keep creative scrapbooks and notebooks where you paste up or jot down creative thoughts from every possible source for future reference and action.

Tune in on Infinite Intelligence, the mightiest Source of all, which you may contact through meditation and prayer.

Creative Computer

THE COMPUTER IS A tool designed by creative think-ers. It can accumulate information on any subject under the sun. It can arrange the material, organize it, control it, and make it instantly available to solve millions of problems that formerly required years of effort.

But only you are a *creative* computer, designed by God.

Your memory bank is as wide as your mind, as deep as your heart, and as high as your vision. It stores a lifetime of impressions from childhood, youth, middle age, and older years—nothing is lost. Peak experiences are there, along with memories of roaring seas, quiet streams, and majestic mountaintops. You carry within you a record of words read and heard; quotations, plays, great books, inspiring poems, majestic music. Everything is tucked away in your mind.

You are the master of your creative computer. You control your own input; the thoughts you think make you what you are. Your philosophy of life is your own creation. You are a computer that is aware of itself. You are unique, extraordinary, and truly creative!

You are the only computer that is both human and divine. You are God's computer, and keeping open to God's input will stimulate your evolution toward being the person you are intended to be. God will pour into you His love, wisdom, and inspiration. God utilizes you to let Himself into the world, as you. Within the miracle of your mind things are always going on. New patterns are being woven, new dreams being dreamt, new concepts being formed, new ideas being born, and answers to eternal riddles are being discovered.

Creative Consciousness

WILLIAM JAMES, the father of modern psychology, gave us the concept of the "stream of consciousness." This stream abounds in all things—images and patterns, facts and figures, hopes and dreams, victory and defeat, laughter and tears; and in all values—good and evil, worthiness and unworthiness, truth and error.

As masters of our destiny, we can stand guard at the Doorway of our Mind and, to a great extent, determine what enters our experience from the stream of consciousness. We can accept the good, reject the bad. Accept the worthy, reject the unworthy. By being open and receptive to the highest and best, and by seeking it out, we can bring to ourselves a vast amount of goodness and energy. We can cause our memory and our subconscious mind to be a savings bank of creative consciousness, filled with vast amounts of priceless data and inspiration.

Expanding your creative consciousness requires a constant attitude of openness, awareness, and searching. You must be constantly alert to what is going on

24

around you. You must make a perpetual effort to stretch the scope and the range of your thinking.

There are tools that you can use in this process. Read widely, and read everything. Keep a file of articles and information from magazines and newspapers. Get into the notebook habit and jot down thoughts and ideas as they come to you. Keep a looseleaf binder of ideas, ideals, philosophies, wisdom, speeches, and poems. Start and continue a journal of your own thoughts and observations.

Developing your creative consciousness will increase the links patterns, connections, formulas, and thoughts you will have available to draw upon in meeting today's problems.

By investing in your creative consciousness, you can become a mental millionaire!

Creative Courage

FOR MANY YEARS I have been collecting books on creative thinking, finally passing them on to Michigan State University. I was pleased recently to have a letter from one of the advertising professors there telling me that his students were surprised to find so much knowledge and inspiration in the writings of what they called *"the creative thinking pioneers."*

As for me I have gone right on reading the newer books on creative thinking—books that are coming out in greater number these days.

One of the best of them is *The Courage to Create*, by the well known philosopher, Rollo May. In my opinion, he has identified the greatest quality a creative thinker can possess: Courage. *"Courage,"* he writes, *"is not a virtue or value among other personal values like love or fidelity. It is the foundation that underlies and gives reality to all other virtues and personal values."*

Courage is the quality that keeps a creative thinker going even through failure and despair, for if he doesn't keep going he will not survive. I often think of the tremendous courage Carlyle had when the completed manuscript of his book about the French Revolution was accidentally destroyed in the fireplace. He mustered the power to sit down and rewrite the entire book!

Visiting Jack London's home in California and reading some of his notes, I was amazed to learn that he had received over six hundred rejection slips before he was finally published.

The same thing goes for inventions of all kinds. They were not just bright ideas. It took courage to stick with those ideas and see them through. Automobiles, airplanes, radio, television, farm equipment—in every area of innovation, failure after failure had to be overcome.

Rollo May also mentions the philosophical theologian Paul Tillich, who wrote the book, *Courage To Be.* Tillich said that we should be a part of the larger whole, involved in human relationships; that we should have the courage to be ourselves and stand alone as an individual person. And finally, that we should be sustained by the creative power of God.

Indeed, it takes courage to create ideas and to make them live and serve.

Creative Daring

WHEN I GO TO A circus, I am thrilled most by the aerialists . . . those daring flyers who swing high on a trapeze and then launch themselves into space to be caught by another aerialist hanging by his or her knees on an opposite trapeze. Recently, I watched a man who is said to be the first person to ever successfully make a triple somersault *and a twist* as he flew through the air to the catcher on the other trapeze!

Circus acrobats are always daring to do something different; they have the courage to attempt the impossible. The creative adventure of their lives is to do something in their particular profession that has never been done before—and then to keep doing it! If a flyer misses their catcher and falls to the net below, or if they fail in a new trick, they don't give up. If they're really good, they climb up the rope ladder to the platform, take off into the air, and try again!

What can creative people learn from this? How about more somersaults and twists in your thinking? How about taking a perilous flight through mental space by doing some different thinking? How about standing on your head and seeing the world from a new angle? How about trying to think of something that has never been thought of before? It may be difficult, but it can also be simple. A good example is that of the man who took a piece of plain wire and twisted it into a paperclip. How many billions of those do you think have been sold?

Today's world needs change, alteration, renewal, and corrections of errors. It needs new ideas, new approaches, methods, plans, procedures, and new ways of doing things. Maybe you should think of going—literally or symbolically—to a circus today, where you'll see stunts you never dreamed possible. The novelty and originality there may stimulate what you need more of in this life. Have the daring to take a flight for the idea you believe in!

Creative Dreams

WHILE YOU ARE sound asleep in your bed, you may have a creative adventure that will change your life or even your world.

Someone has said that dreams are *"God's forgotten language."* Today dreams are being rediscovered as a powerful creative force, and in many different fields of activity dreams have already made great contributions.

A cornerstone of modern chemistry was discovered by the German chemist Friedrich Kekule when he dreamed of a snake swallowing its own tail and suddenly conceived of the ring-like structure of the benzene molecule.

Elias Howe, inventor of the sewing machine, had a nightmare about cannibals with holes in their spears and was inspired to solve the problem of creating a practical mechanical needle.

Dreaming of a horse race caused Niels Bohr to imagine that electrons travel in fixed "lanes" around a nucleus.

It is said that Einstein got his first insight into relativity when he dreamt of speeding down a hill on a sled.

Mozart would often arise early in the morning to set down some melody he had dreamed of in the night.

For almost 20 years, Harriet Beecher Stowe witnessed the abuses and suffering caused by slavery, but she found no way to express her sympathies until 1851 when she was sitting in a church in Brunswick, Maine. In a trance or dream-like state, she saw the image of a white man forcing two slaves to flog to death an old black man. She could almost hear the old man praying as he died.

Later that day, Stowe began writing *Life Among the Lowly* or *Uncle Tom's Cabin*, the book that galvanized support for the abolition of slavery and ultimately led to the American Civil War.

Many authors receive ideas and themes for their stories through dreams. Stevenson said that the complete plot for his classic *Dr. Jekyll and Mr. Hyde* came to him in a dream.

In my personal experience, during my teens, I had a dream in which I saw a book I had authored, in a spotlight, with my name on the cover in large letters. I'm not sure if a title was shown, but later in one of my boyhood notebooks I found these words: *"Someday I will write a book of 'Little Essays on Living.'"*

One thing all dream experts agree upon is that when you have a dream, you should wake up and immediately write it down. Otherwise it may be gone forever. So keep a notebook at your bedside.

It was a wise man who said, *"A dream that has not been interpreted is like a letter that has not been opened."*

Creative Evolution

CREATIVE EVOLUTION means an evolution which you personally create. The secret of creative evolution is to break through your inertia barrier and GET STARTED: to overcome the challenges of difficulties and obstacles and continue to move forward physically, mentally and spiritually.

Aldous Huxley put it this way: *"Perhaps the most valuable result of education is the ability to make yourself do the thing you have to do, when it has to be done, whether you like it or not."*

Conscious evolution applies to the whole person —body, mind, heart and spirit. And we are not in competition with anyone but ourselves. Our only challenge: How can *I* become better?

I've always been impressed with what the New Testament has to say about Jesus when it leaves him as a boy of twelve years and does not return to him again until he is a full-grown man entering upon his ministry. It gives a key to the creative evolution of his greatness in a single sentence. It indicates that he creatively evolved in four areas: *"He increased in wisdom and stature and in favor with God and man."*

As Jesus creatively evolved during those eighteen years of preparation for his life work, I believe that the wisdom he discovered are in these words: *"Seek ye first the Kingdom of God and His righteousness and all these things shall be added unto you."*

Creative evolution is a process that continues through a whole lifetime. It is seeking always the kingdom of great and noble thoughts. It is cultivating inner harmony, balanced behavior, outgoing love and enduring peace. It is affirming day after day, again and again, the words of the French mystic: *"Day by day, in every way, I'm getting better and better."*

Creative Family

THERE IS NO POWER in earth, heaven, nor the universe that can keep you from having a happy home if you think and create.

Give your home the creative touch. Gardens, flowers, hammocks, trees, beauty, and relaxation OUTSIDE; paintings, photographs, mottos, books, music, games, toys, inspiration, and fun INSIDE.

The result will be dynamic magnetic power that will attract and hold everyone.

Rediscover the family and let joy abound. Be creative heroes and heroines for your children. Champion goodness, imagination, originality, progress, and success. Pray to be loving and useful.

Give your family a creative education. Organize a family creative thinking team, with mother and dad as coaches. Hold a creative session once a week. Expect everyone to come up with ideas on everything. Make me. You'll be delighted by the response.

Have a "Log Book" and appoint someone to keep a record of the ideas you spark. Appoint group members and committees to put the ideas to work. Fresh, new creative thinking will spur you on.

Watch your children for creative potential. Growing up in your family may be poets, novelists, dramatists, engineers, researchers, social workers, musicians, ministers, or even a future president of the United States.

Learning to be creative thinkers will help them on their way!

Creative Fantasy

To ENTER THE kingdom of ideas, become as a little child.

"There is nothing more resembles God's eyes," wrote Nikos Kazantzakis, *"than the eyes of a child."*

A child does not block the flow of goodness into his life by thoughts of fear and prejudice. His mind is as open as his eyes. He experiences the wonder of life.

A child lives in the world of fantasy, where all great ideas are born. It was probably a child who first dreamed of flying through the air, of hearing music from the sky. A child believes in fairies and in magic lamps.

A child is an explorer. He or she is curious and is constantly asking, *"Why?"* He or she loves to experiment.

A child has the gift of imagination. He or she may see things that aren't there. They create in their minds the kind of world they want to live in. Each child visualizes his or her self as many different personalities —a doctor, lawyer, dancer, poet, pilot, singer . . .

A child has freshness of response. The world is ever new and full of miracles and adventures. The child greets each new discovery of the day with joy and enthusiasm.

A child follows the simple way. Not bogged down by the complex and obscure, he or she seeks the obvious in a natural, direct, and sincere manner.

A child is confident. He or she believes in their ability, because they have not learned all the reasons why things cannot be done. Obstacles are ignored because a child doesn't know that they exist. To a child everything is possible.

Children have much to teach us about creativity. Usually the more childlike we are in our approach to problems the more creative we will be.

So why not try the creative approach of a child?

Creative Flow

IN MY 84TH YEAR, Aquinas College celebrated my writing career by awarding me an honorary Doctor of Humane Letters degree.

In accepting the degree with deep appreciation, I went on to say that the words I have written did not come from me, but came *through* me instead. I served only as a channel for their flow.

Where did the ideas and inspiration come from? From universal sources—from a star, a tree, a friend, a stranger, a child, a mountain, a sunny meadow, the sea. From books and talks and sermons. From a symphony or a folk song. From crowds and solitude. From the whisperings of God's love and goodness.

A writer's task, I pointed out, is to tune in on life, to keep open, receptive and aware. A writer, I suggested, should not wait for inspiration, but should begin writing. The images and words are there in your deep inner mind, waiting for you to stimulate their flow through you.

Looking out over the crowd of eager graduates, I stressed the fact that the principle of flow applies to all areas of activity. (But to have something great to give in any field, you must prepare yourself. You must saturate yourself with the highest and the best in the field. Thus you become ready for that flow to emerge through you, to enrich your own life and the lives of others.)

As an aside to you, I note that the flow technique mentioned here is something that I have tried and tested over many years. As near as I can estimate I have so far written close to ten million words in my lifetime, which would make close to 40,000 typed pages. Thus, I testify from my own experience and assure you that when you open yourself to the creative flow of inspiration, you will be rewarded!

Creative Feeling

*F*EELING LIGHTS the fuse for igniting great ideas.

Architect Allen Dow declared that there is a *"feeling word"* at the very heart of creativity. That word is *"care."* To solve a problem, write a book, paint a picture, render a service, or do any other creative thing, we must care enough to put forth a heroic and dedicated effort. We must care enough to throw our whole heart into the task before us. We must truly care if we are to achieve the highest and best. Care fuels the conquering spirit that works miracles.

Care is powerful because it switches our attention from self to others. It is people-oriented. It concentrates not on getting but on giving.

Millions of the world's poor died alone in the streets and byways of the world until one diminutive nun in a white sari began going into the streets of Calcutta to gather up the dying and care for them. Now Mother Teresa's work is carried on all around the world. Her message of love and caring was heard when she accepted the Nobel Peace Prize in 1979.

John Dewey gives further evidence of the importance of feeling in creative thinking. He wrote that the first step is to seek to discover what he called *"felt difficulties."* This suggests that we should look for human needs, and then creatively fill those needs. This is the secret of success in business. Only when a difficulty or need is deeply felt will we be stimulated and aroused to think deeply about it. Ideas come to us when we desperately feel the need for them and turn the world upside down to find them.

Care involves a broad emotional approach to creativity. Caring is the mark of creative greatness in every area of our lives. Discovering "felt difficulties" pinpoints specific areas for intense concentration. Working with both "caring" and with "felt difficulties" are ways of battling the chief enemies of creativity, inertia and complacency—and of using the power of feeling to create a better world.

Creative Freedom

COME! LET US celebrate creative freedom.

This country was designed and built by creative thinkers. There were brilliant fireworks in the words that Jefferson wrote in the Declaration of Independence. Thomas Paine penned sparks of inspiration to keep the soldier's spirits up. Behind it all was the organizational strategy of Alexander Hamilton. Leading the troops to victory was the gallant George Washington. Helping to create the constitution of the new nation was the elder statesman, Ben Franklin. Heroes of creative freedom, every one!

Creative freedom is the secret power that has made our nation great. It is also the key to continued greatness.

Creative freedom means freedom for the individual.

Her mother had taught her to believe in freedom in America but the realities of Rosa Park's life in Montgomery, Alabama in 1951 fell short of her mother's dreams.

Weary after making alterations all day in a department store, Parks boarded the bus for home. Seated behind the white passengers, she was later asked to relinquish her seat to a white man who boarded the bus.

Her reply, *"I don't think I have to,"* triggered her arrest and a 381-day bus boycott in Montgomery which renewed the struggle for civil rights in the United States.

You are free to act on your own account and you do not have to wait for others to change before you do. You are free to change yourself, to do your own thinking, to create new ideas. The world is waiting for your creative gifts to be expressed. Freedom is an open door but you must walk through it. Freedom is a mountain and you must climb it.

Creative freedom is an inner freedom. It removes mental and emotional chains and liberates your best self. It inspires you to stand tall, radiating confidence. It spurs you on to fulfill yourself, to make your dreams come true.

Creative freedom, when you exercise it, is your personal key to a stimulating and fulfilling life.

Creative Future

I VISUALIZE YOU standing on top of a mountain, reaching for the sky!

This mystical mountain is made up of all the knowledge, wisdom and experiences accumulated by humanity since time began. The successes, the achievements, the failures, the losses, the defeats are all there. The discoveries: fire, the wheel, the telescope, the microscope, electricity, plus the rapidly multiplying number of other civilization-changing developments and inventions. The works of great creative men and women who left their marks to inspire you: scientists, prophets, preachers, teachers, poets, philosophers, historians, statesmen, composers, authors, engineers, painters, sculptors—the extraordinary procession of human genius. You have the richest legacy of creativity that anyone has ever had.

You, standing on the mystical mountaintop and reaching for the sky, have more creative power at your fingertips today than has been available at any other time in history.

In the years to come, you will face an unfinished world. Nothing is done finally and completely. The creative horizon is aglow with new things to do. Peace is always a shining possibility. Hunger and poverty are still to be conquered. Freedom and happiness are still positive goals to be attained. And you will have the opportunity to apply the whole knowledge of humanity to these great issues—*plus* your own creativity, your own genius.

Historian Arnold Toynbee advances the theory of "challenge and response." *"Civilization only advances"*, he writes, *"when the environment is just right to issue a challenge to the people and when they are ready to respond to it . . ."*

Creative Genie

M Y DICTIONARY describes a genie as a supernatural being who does one's bidding, a guardian spirit. We may wonder: Is the genie only a myth or does he represent something real? Might "genie" mean the subconscious mind, intuition, the inner self, the God within? Did Jesus, when he said, *"The Father that dwelleth within me, he doeth the works,"* refer to what others call a genie?

When an idea strikes you in the middle of the night, or while you are out for a walk, is it your genie nudging you? (In a survey of creative people, it was discovered that their best ideas did not come to them while they were at their desks, but came instead in their time off, while they were loafing.)

One of the wonderful things about genies is that they work while we sleep. Given a problem before you go to bed, you'll often find that when you wake up, your genie has supplied the answer you need.

Recently I had a letter from a friend who told me that he belongs to a "Genie Club," a group of people who get together to tell what their respective genies have done for them—to explore the whole idea of genie activity. Socrates once said, *"I must answer to my genie."* Perhaps all of his wise philosophy about "know thyself" was stimulated by that relationship. Ruskin said, *"Greatness does not come from great men, but through them."* Maybe he was suggesting that a genie was at work.

There is much study of mythology going on today and myths are being found to have deep spiritual significance. Perhaps there is also much to find out about genies and how they work.

How about doing a little experimenting yourself, and becoming better acquainted with your genie? Make him or her your partner in creative projects. Outline your problems and then be alert to how your genie answers.

Remember that Aladdin and his Magic Lamp did all right. Isn't it worthwhile to give your own genie a try?

Creative Giving

T HESE WORDS FROM Albert Schweitzer changed my
life, and they may change yours: *"You are happy.
Therefore you are called to give up much. Whatever you
have received more than others in health, in talents, in ability, in a pleasant childhood, in harmonious conditions of
home life, all this you must not take to yourself as a matter of course. You must pay for it. You must render in return
an unusually great sacrifice of your life for other lives."*

Clara McBride Hale, or "Mother Hale" as she is
called, loves children and when she began finding
abused, abandoned, and even infants infected with the
AIDS virus, she took them in and loved them as her
own.

In 1969, Mother Hale opened Hale House, a shelter
for children and a lifesaving environment for young
drug-addicted mothers. In recognition of her contribution, President Ronald Reagan named Mother Hale an
American Hero in 1985.

An attitude of creative giving can become the
greatest creative force in the world. When we consider
all that others have done for us since the world began
we become stimulated and inspired to do something for
the world. In a deep sense we owe the world a creative

spirit. There are millions of ways, great and small, that creative energy may be put to work.

Success in life is too often measured by what a person acquires. More meaningful is what a person contributes.

And this goes beyond the contribution of money to the contribution of ideas, plans, methods, ideals, visions, projects. Behind all material progress is mental and spiritual progress. The creative thinkers start the ball rolling. They visualize programs and goals. They dream dreams. They help people to grow.

And in a personal way they enrich themselves in something more than dollars. They contribute love, hope, courage, faith, peace, and joy to others. Such a spirit of contribution has broad and long-lasting influence; a depth of true success is experienced that can be attained in no other way.

Go-givers are far more effective than go-getters, and when you give ideas, you give the most precious gifts life has to offer, for everything begins with an idea!

Creative Gold

A FRIEND OF mine made a wise observation the other day. He told me: *"I no longer pay much attention to what a person says. I simply watch how he or she lives."*

We are all "walking philosophies," representing outwardly what we really are inside. We are bundles of impressions, made up of our attitudes, feelings, thoughts and actions. We become that which has influenced us the most, and often chance seems to play a great part in determining what that is.

There is a way, however, that we can reduce the extent to which chance seems to determine who we are and be more creative in building our philosophies. A clue to this creative approach came to my wife and me while visiting Alaska. At a forty-year-old gold mine, we were given pans and told to go down to a stream and pan for gold. Again and again, we dipped into the stream, filled the pan with water, and whirled it around. Among the sand and gravel we finally found grains of gold.

The awareness came to us as we worked that life is a stream. William James, in fact, called it a *"stream of consciousness."* It is full of mental sand and gravel, but it also contains grains of gold, and if we are lucky there may even be golden nuggets. Creating a positive and constructive philosophy depends on seeking the highest and best in life and making it a part of our thinking and living.

I will always remember one thing that Herb Engstrom, owner of the mine, said, *"Gold won't come and kiss you. You have to work for it."*

And that is also true of the gold of living, isn't it?

Creative Gratitude

CREATIVE GRATITUDE IS AN attitude. It is magnetic and will draw good to you. It is good therapy, a road to happiness.

Thankfulness is a way of living more fully. Be thankful for your health and you will have health in more abundance. Be thankful for the love you receive and it will be increased. Be thankful for your success and you'll open doors to further achievement. Be thankful for your friends and more friends will come to you. Be thankful for beauty and you'll experience it more deeply.

Thankfulness is a way of enhancing relationships. Expressions of gratitude create in others an eagerness to reciprocate. When we become more fully aware that our success is due in large measure to the loyalty, helpfulness, and encouragement we have received from others, our desire grows to pass on similar gifts. Gratitude spurs us on to prove ourselves worthy of what others have done for us. The spirit of gratitude is a powerful energizer.

Thankfulness is a way of worshipping. All through

the Psalms the emphasis is on thankfulness: *"Sing to the Lord with thanksgiving"* . . . *"Let us come before His presence with thanksgiving"* . . . *"O give thanks unto the Lord, for He is good; for His steadfast love endures forever"* . . . *"I will give thanks to the Lord with my whole heart."*

When Jesus healed the ten lepers only one returned to fall at the feet of the Master and give thanks to God. With this in mind someone has written that nine were healed, while the one who gave thanks was made whole. The expression of gratitude made the big difference.

Creative gratitude is a force for harmony and goodwill. It brings people together in love and understanding. It is high on the scale of creative qualities to be practiced day in and day out in our moment-to-moment contacts.

Creative Growth

RECENTLY, I TURNED ninety. I did not suddenly become wise. I saw no visions. I discovered that all I am and all I know is the result of the accumulated knowledge and experience of the time before I became ninety. Every day, every week, every month, every year made its contribution to my life.

A man's philosophy isn't something that comes to him "out of the blue" on his ninetieth birthday, or at any other time. It is not an entirely new illumination or revelation. Rather, it is the sum total of the life he has lived—his thoughts, his deeds, his creative adventures. The influences that have been poured into his mind and spirit have made him what he is. Life has fashioned him into a living, walking philosophy.

The keys to growth are available to us the day we are born. They include openness, sensitivity, awareness, insight, intuition, wonder, imagination, curiosity, empathy, compassion, and creativity. These keys will unlock the doors to a rich life. What I am at ninety or what you are at your age, depends upon how we use these keys.

Our philosophy will change and mature with the years as a new light and understanding come to us, and we must maintain a seeking attitude. Philosophy is not static. It is dynamic. It is constantly expanding and unfolding. So think of the evolution of your philosophy as a great adventure. Look everywhere. Read everything. Listen to everyone. Meditate. Pray. Live. Search for meaning. Be aware that today you are creating your tomorrow. Use the events and opportunities to build a personal philosophy of high vision and sensible living. Don't think you have to wait for wisdom.

Creative Happiness

THE CONVENTIONAL Happy New Year approach is to think of the New Year as something that happens *outside* of ourselves. It is a good luck wish that the New Year, in some magical way, will *bring us* health, happiness, peace, and success. We look at the New Year to *make* us happy.

Haven't you discovered, as I have, that when we expect happiness from the *outside* we are usually disappointed? We find that happiness is not guaranteed by sunny weather, a raise in pay, a new home, or anything else of a material nature.

Happiness does not come out of a year, it comes out of men and women. Life does not change with the turning of a calendar page. The only way life will change for us is when we *change ourselves*. Happiness is not so much the result of events happening *outside* of us as it is the result of thoughts and emotions going on *inside* of us. We cannot control world events but we can control our own minds and hearts. And true happiness is an inner experience.

I would like to suggest a new phrase that we can speak to each other as we face the adventure of a New Year . . . "HAPPY NEW YOU!"

The way for you to make the New Year the best year in your life is to approach it as a *new person*:

✳ *To think of yourself as being reborn in your thinking and feeling.*

✳ *To leave old thoughts, old habits, old viewpoints behind and enter into a new way of life.*

✳ *To look to yourself, not to the coming months, for your happiness.*

Creative Heart

"*B*LESSED ARE THE *pure in heart for they shall see God.*"

In an age that so reveres the accomplishments of the intellect, has the wisdom of the heart been forgotten? The eleventh-century philosopher, Ansari of Herat, recognized the proper priority of the heart when he wrote, "*Can you walk on water? You have done no better than a straw. Can you fly in the air? You have done no better than a bluebottle. Conquer your heart; then you can be somebody.*"

Confucius further indicated the manner in which the heart influences the nature of the world: "*If there is righteousness in the heart, there will be beauty in the character and harmony in the home, there will be order in the nation. Where there is order in the nation, there will be peace in the world.*"

It is not through the conquest of things, but the

conquest of the heart that leads us to a richer life. Draw up an inventory of all your feelings from hate to love, and you will discover the rating of your heart. How do we conquer our heart? By rejecting negative values in favor of positive ones. By opening our heart to the needs of others. By letting the heart as well as the mind examine a problem. By giving the heart the authority to make us more aware and sensitive to life around us.

We do not need to walk on water or fly higher or faster. We need to conquer our heart. This is the great accomplishment the Ancients have been telling us about for centuries. It is time we listened to them . . . with our hearts.

Creative Heroes

FOR MANY YEARS, I have had on the walls of my study, where I can see them every day, portraits of my four creative heroes, people who have been a constant inspiration to me.

First, there is Jesus, in H. Stanley Todd's painting *The Triumphant Nazarene*, which shows Jesus as the dynamic, magnetic personality he must have been. It always brings to my mind three of the basic statements of Jesus: *"I and my Father are one,"* *"The Kingdom of God is within you,"* and *"Suffer little children to come unto me . . . for of such is the Kingdom of God."*

Second, there is a portrait of Lincoln as President. This often brings to my mind a brief statement he made on how to become a great writer: *"Always write so a child will understand, then no one will misunderstand."* Born in a log cabin, and having had only a few years of schooling, Lincoln nevertheless wrote two masterpieces, the *Gettysburg Address* and the *Second Inaugural*.

Third is a portrait of Ralph Waldo Emerson. A hundred years after his death, Emerson is still the most quoted writer in America. In my own writing, Emerson's ideas seem to blend spontaneously with mine, and I find myself unconsciously using them. I owe him a great debt, and I have even built my writings around this one idea of Emerson: *"Set down nothing that will not help somebody."*

Fourth is a photograph of Elbert Hubbard, given to me by his son. Hubbard was a real force in America at the turn of the century, though now he seems to be in limbo. Few remember him. But I am an all-out Hubbard fan: he wrote with vigor and wit, and I admire his skill. His writings are still available. Discover them and you will be amazed and inspired.

My appreciation of these four portraits is only part of my plan to saturate myself with the thoughts and lives of these men. Reading is another part. In addition to various translations of the New Testament, I have read many studies of Jesus and interested myself in comparative religion. I have collected thirty biographies of Lincoln; I have the complete writings of Emerson and Hubbard and all the biographies of them I can find. I try to live with my heroes.

My suggestion to you is that you find your own heroes and hang their portraits in your home or office. Then read books about them and keep notebooks of their wisdom.

Creative Ideals

ALL MY LIFE I have been a "hunt and peck" typist, so I make my share of errors. The other day a strange thing happened. Intending to type the word *"idea,"* I hit an extra letter and wrote *"ideal."* Serendipity at work!

When you stop to think about it, ideas themselves can be either moral or immoral; they can promote good causes or bad, quality products or inferior ones.

But add an "l" to idea and you create "ideal", and ideals are always on the side of the angels. The letter "l" tips the scale toward the good, the honest, the upright. The letter "l" writes figures in black ink, on the credit side of the moral and spiritual ledger. When we turn *idea* into *ideal*, it goes to work to help build a better world.

Creative idealism represents the combined power of mind and spirit. It becomes a dynamic expression of the goodness of God. Ideas that work for peace, brotherhood, freedom, happiness, prosperity, health, growth . . . these deserve the extra letter "l", for they are truly creative ideals.

As I have pointed out many times, the final step in creative thinking is *verification*, when we evaluate ideas. We try to consider them in terms of their true worth (the Golden Rule is one good standard to use). Are the ideas true, genuine, and worthy of you?

When we evaluate ideas in terms of ideals we upgrade them. We discover new values, deeper meanings, inspiring objectives. We begin to aim our thinking higher.

Ideas clothed in the shining robes of ideals are glorified. They go marching forth to bless and benefit.

Creative Idea-Trapping

ONCE AN IDEA illuminates your mind, catch it immediately with an idea-trap. An idea-trap is made up of pencil and paper. Get into the notebook habit. Have a notebook by your favorite chair. By your bed. In your pocket. Once you have an idea come to you, do not let it escape. Capture it immediately, trap it, write it down.

The Chinese have a proverb: *"The strongest memory is weaker than the palest ink."*

Millions of ideas are lost to the world every year, when we fail to write them down as they flash in our minds.

The moment a great idea hits, it is so bright and shining we are sure we will remember it forever. But we only fool ourselves, for we may not be able to recall it tomorrow. It will have escaped, never to return.

The advertising business is largely the business of ideas. Over my forty years in that business I lost a fortune in ideas, many of which came in the middle of the night. I knew I should get up and trap them with pencil and paper and often I did just that. But there were other times when I told myself the idea was so good, I was sure I would remember it . . . and I turned over and went back to sleep. In the morning the idea was gone with the wind.

In my talks on creative thinking, I often told about the doctor who saved millions of lives by getting up in the night and writing down an idea. The doctor was Frederick Grant Banting. After a day of research he went to bed exhausted. About two a.m. he awoke, struggled to get up, and wrote a note to himself. In the morning he remembered writing the note but forgot what he had written. He took a look and saw: *"Tie off the pancreatic ducts of dogs. Wait six or eight weeks for degeneration. Remove residue and extract."* It was the key to the discovery of insulin!

Ideas are like gold or precious stones; their value is without price. Never take a chance. Trap every one!

Creative Imagination

I MAGINATION IS A flame that ignites the creative spirit. Imagination lights up your mind by stoking mental fires. It can be stimulated from the outside through the senses, or from the inside through the driving power of curiosity and discontent.

Imagination stimulates your thinking power by giving your mind abundant data with which to work. It opens the gate to dreams and fantasies so that you may become receptive, as a little child, in exploring the Kingdom of Ideas.

Imagination guides you in your contacts with individuals and crowds, so you can discover creative sparks to help you develop new concepts and approaches.

Imagination inspires you to look at everything with fresh eyes, as though you had just come forth from a dark tunnel into the light of day. Imagination becomes for you a magic lamp with which to search the darkness of the unknown, that you may discover new goals or chart more productive paths to old goals.

Imagination helps you to recognize the reality of facts, but then to go beyond them, to penetrate beneath them, to rise above them in your search for creative answers to problems. Imagination *"stirs up the gift of God in thee."* Through your imagination you touch and express the inspiration of the Infinite. Imagination, in the words of Shakespeare, *"gives to airy nothing a local habitation and a name."* You reach into the heavens to grasp an idea, then you bring it down to earth and make it work.

Creative Inspiration

M Y FRIEND, the late Joseph Sadony—a scientist, philosopher, and mystic—writing in his autobiography, had this to say about inspiration: "*Of course inspiration is nothing but your imagination. But your imagination will tell you the truth if you seek with a prayer (tuning in), and if you will stop thinking with your brain and offer up every nerve, from the top of your head to the tips of your fingers and toes, for inspiration. What is inspiration? First it is a 'feeling' and then the feeling sings a song, writes a book, or solves a problem that changes the course of history.*"

I like that! I've found that inspiration is the spark which starts the engine of creativity. Be aware, sensitive, and alert to inspiration, and when it comes put it to work. Keep your spiritual antenna reaching for inspiration, for nothing great was ever accomplished without it.

I have discovered four things that stimulate inspiration for me, and may do so for you.

First, keep a scrapbook of good and great thoughts. Seeking the good will lift your consciousness. Emerson said he hesitated before throwing away the smallest scrap of paper without looking at both sides, *"lest it should contain some thought, or fact or verse worthy of preservation."*

Second, since many things you want to keep will appear on both sides of the paper, copy that material in a loose-leaf notebook. Also include condensations of sermons, speeches, and books.

Third, keep a journal of your own experiences, travels, adventures, and thoughts. Through the years it will become a gold mine.

Fourth, build a library of inspirational books. (An inspirational book I read when I was sixteen— *Leadership* by George N. Knox—changed my life.)

These four things have given me a lifetime of inspiration. I'm sure they will do the same for you.

Creative Instrument

In Carl Sandburg's biography of Abraham Lincoln there is a chapter on Lincoln's humor and religion. Sandburg tells about a conversation between two Quaker women during the Civil War. They were speaking of Jefferson Davis, the President of the Confederacy, and their conversation went like this:

"I think Jefferson will succeed."
"Why does thee think so?"
"Because Jefferson is a praying man."
"And so is Abraham a praying man."
"Yes, but the Lord will think Abraham is joking."

Lincoln was never one to tell God what to do. Instead he opened himself to God's creative power and made himself an instrument of the will of God.

On one occasion Lincoln said, *"I claim not to have controlled events, but confess plainly that events have controlled me."*

Those who knew Lincoln well said that his method was to get himself in the right place and remain there, still and receptive, until events would find him in that place. He let things build up until the time for action came and he felt God had shown him what to do.

In his four-volume study, *Lincoln the President*, J.G.

Randall has one whole chapter titled, "God's Man." He writes of Lincoln's strange dreams and his mystic affinity for the Quakers, of his Universalist and Unitarian views, and of his regular participation in Presbyterian services. He concludes with this sentence: *"Indeed Lincoln was a man of more intense religiosity than any other President the United States ever had."*

Long ago, before presidents had a whole staff of ghost-writers as they have today, Lincoln wrote his own speeches and they included such masterpieces as the Gettysburg Address and the Second Inaugural Address. God was certainly inspiring him to write these Immortal words . . .

"With malice toward none, with charity for all; with firmness in the right, as God gives us to see the right, let us strive on to finish the work we are in, to bind up the nation's wounds; to care for him who shall have borne the battle, and for his widow, and his orphan—to do all which may achieve and cherish a just and lasting peace, among ourselves, and with all nations."

Creative Intuition

I T HAS BEEN around a long time and has been called by many names; a hunch, a lucky guess, a feeling in the bones, an answer to prayer. Edison spoke of it as *"listening within."* The late Leo Burnett, considered one of the greatest thinkers in the history of the advertising business, called it *"creative conscience."*

Today the concept has been rediscovered, and psychologists, spiritual leaders, and business experts are writing books about it. There is a growing wave of interest in *intuition!*

As a young woman, Florence Nightingale turned away suitors and almost intuitively concentrated her efforts on studying health and reforms in Paris and later in Germany.

Nightingale was a highly intelligent woman with a rare ability for organization. The Crimean War provided her with the ultimate challenge. Known as the "Lady With the Lamp," Nightingale walked the miles of hospital wards comforting the wounded. Although she was going against the conventions of her day, Nightingale instinctively knew that health care could be improved.

She later became a recognized authority on the scientific care of the medical patients. For her efforts, Nightingale became the first woman to ever be awarded the British Order of Merit.

My dictionary defines intuition as *"the act or faculty*

of knowing without the use of rational processes; immediate cognition; a capacity for guessing accurately; sharp insight." Intuition is no doubt the greatest creative tool we have because it reaches higher and digs deeper than any other factor. Women especially have demonstrated this power.

To his creative people, Leo Burnett wrote, *"In every one of you there is a wee small voice in the back of your mind. You might call it your 'creative conscience.' To be really creative you have to listen to that voice, to trust it, and to act on what it tells you."*

While "literary lions" scoffed that women knew nothing of life, writers like Jane Austen, the Bronte Sisters, Pearl Buck, Willa Cather, Alice Walker, and Virginia Woolf have meticulously laid bare the human condition.

To have intuition speak its magic words, to answer your problem or provide the big idea you seek, simply follow the creative thinking process I have often written about. First, fill your mind with data about the subject. Then, allow this material to simmer in your subconscious mind while you turn to other things. Before you fall asleep at night go over the material and again turn it over to your subconscious, confident that your intuition will have the answer for you in the morning. Or if the answer doesn't come in the morning, you might go for a walk with an open and receptive mind and an expectant attitude. (All through the Bible we are advised to *"wait on the Lord"*). If you have done your "homework", if you stored away the data, the answer will come. So, wait with Faith!

Creative Journal

"*THE PURPOSE OF LIFE,*" said Emerson, "*is to acquaint man with himself.*" Keeping a journal for fifty years helped Emerson do that. I liked the idea and kept a journal myself. Doing so has been a big help to me and will help you, too!

On August 21, 1964, for example, I recorded these observations on creative writing:

"I have been told that I should relax and let the creative Spirit flow through me. But I find that the Spirit needs effort on my part to start the flow going. I must try. I must work to start the flow. I must start my cold mental machine working. I'm convinced that the only way to write is to start writing . . . thus I open the door for inspiration."

When I am not writing I must be preparing to write. I must keep myself sensitive, aware, and alert. Writing is not just the act of pounding a typewriter. It means reading widely, keeping notes, observing, traveling, talking with people, meditating, praying. (As I meditate, I have experienced receiving an idea so powerful that it has driven me to the typewriter where I cannot set the words down fast enough.)

On one occasion, I recorded Alexis Carrel's words about the writer's (and perhaps everybody's) greatest enemy—inertia:

"Life leaps like a geyser for those who drill through the rock of inertia."

In 1964, when I retired at age 65, I wrote the following in my journal: *"I pray that these retirement years will be the most creative years of my entire life. This I know will require dedication and discipline, but I'm going to give it a whirl!"*

75

Creative Joy

J OY ACCELERATES creativity!

"*Never write to pay a bill,*" is what the poet Robert Frost told a group of eager beavers seeking the secret of being writers. Money as a motive freezes creativity. Joy, on the other hand, causes creativity to flow. We should consider everything we write as a joyful gift to the reader—an idea, entertainment, beauty, idealism, adventure, wisdom. Try giving yourself away in the words you write; such words have magnetic power to draw readers.

Once I drove to Camden, New Jersey, to visit the home of Walt Whitman. In 1884, he bought a home there for $1,750—a group of wooden, two-story houses joined together, which is now the headquarters of the Walt Whitman Association. Here are old manuscripts, letters, and photographs. Walt's hobby was collecting photographs, mostly of himself, although, the hostess told us, "Walt didn't spend much time in the house. He loved to be out mingling with people." He once said: "*People are so much sunshine to the square inch.*" His one great book, *Leaves of Grass*, started out with 12 poems, while the final edition, published in 1892, contains almost 400 poems. Every poem was on the same subject—the joy of being human.

Tolstoy wrote what many consider to be the world's greatest novel, *War and Peace*. The manuscript, all written with a pen, totaled over 5,000 pages. His biographers say of Tolstoy: *"He wrote in a cloud of joy."*

Emily Dickinson, a reclusive, young American genius, found both her joy and her creativity in objects as simple as raindrops, bumble bees, and daffodils.

Someone had said that Mark Twain enjoyed every word he wrote. I'll bet he laughed out loud when he penned this suggestion: *"So live that when you die even the undertaker will be sorry."*

Creative joy is used by great achievers in every field. As Elbert Hubbard wrote, *"Find joy in your work and you'll know what happiness is."*

Creative Kingdom

THE MASTER'S WORDS go to the heart of the matter: *"Neither say Lo here, or Lo there for behold the kingdom of God is within you."*

This inner kingdom is a kingdom of ideals, beauty, wonder, devotion, dedication, and love. It is a kingdom of thoughts and prayers and noble aspirations. It is an invincible kingdom of the spirit. In this kingdom we may commune with those who know its secrets well— the seers, prophets, sages, mystics, philosophers—those great hearts and souls who have discovered the kingdom's inner meanings.

This inner kingdom will enrich creative thinking and lift the ideals and purposes of creative thinkers. More emphasis will be put upon intuition, insight, inspiration, meditation, and matters of the spirit as well as the mind. Thus we will revolutionize creativity and reach for higher projects and goals.

The starting point for the outer kingdom is the inner kingdom. We must see a great light, expand our thinking, lift our consciousness, catch an inner vision, and change ourselves.

An ancient Hindu statement explains the inner kingdom's far-reaching dimensions: *"The spirit within me is greater than the earth and the sky and heaven all united."*

It is not in heaven where we will find people, but in people that we will find heaven. This is the goal of the dedicated creative thinker.

Creative Liberty

To THIS COUNTRY's Founding Fathers, liberty transcended even life itself. Liberty became the very foundation of the new nation, the greatest new idea in government ever created.

Liberty is still the most creative motivating force in America today. A friend of mine, the late James Mangan, had liberty in mind, when he entitled his book, *You Can Do Anything.* And so you can. There are no barriers that will not give way to a conquering spirit. Opportunity is constantly knocking at your door. To quote one line from Jim's inspiring book: *"You can do anything because, when you believe you can, all the power of the gods is working with you and nothing is impossible to your fury and zeal."*

A biographical sketch about James Mangan that appeared at the time his book was published told about a friend who, knowing Jim couldn't write, sing, or whistle a note of music, challenged him to write a song.

Within a week Mangan produced both music and lyrics for a song. And Kate Smith sang his song over the air fifty times. Jim proved he could do anything!

Jim proved himself in other ways, too. For thirty-seven years he was the top-spinner champion of the world. His top-spinning magic was once featured in a *Life Magazine* article.

In a deeper and more universal way, St. Augustine has given us a maxim which expresses what we might call *"cosmic liberty."* He wrote, *"Love and do as you will."* It has often been said that we should think before we speak, but in the light of St. Augustine's philosophy, we should *"Love before we speak"* and *"Love before we act."*

Creative Light

IN FEBRUARY 1987, astronomers made a sensational discovery, when a supernova—an exploding star—burst into view over the southern sky. Not a single supernova had been seen in our galaxy since 1604.

Creative thinking, an explosion of ideas, is powerfully akin to this celestial event. Creativity brings light into every corner of the world. There are big ideas and little ideas, working together to create the magic by which inner darkness disappears. And we can all be a part of this process.

I like the old proverb: *"It is better to light a candle than to curse the darkness."* We need to create a moral and spiritual equivalent to the supernova here on our earth, a super-creativity which will abolish war, which will conquer hunger, poverty, disease, and crime.

Light illuminates, penetrates the darkness, shows the way ahead. Light is synonymous with creativity. It is explosive mental power. It is the mind aflame, the heart aglow, the spirit aware. It is God at work through you.

Charles and Anne Morrow Lindbergh were America's golden couple. Then in March 1932 their young son, Charles Lindbergh, Jr. was kidnapped and brutally murdered.

In her published letters and diary entries, Anne Morrow Lindbergh recounts the tragic months that followed. For her, the light that guided her through the grief was learning how others had come through their trials.

Just as she was indebted to the people who had left behind their testimonies, Anne Morrow Lindbergh believed that in her books she, too, must leave her own *"little grain of truth."* After all, grain must be resown in order to grow.

Goethe's cry, *"More light,"* as he was dying brought a dynamic message to all of us. For this is what we need in every area of life; more inspiration, more love, more tolerance, more understanding, more thinking. More light is the goal of all creative thinkers. It is absolutely limitless in the scope of its possibilities.

Creative Listening

ONE OF THE most important habits of a creative thinker is to be a good listener. Stand guard at the ear-gateway to your mind, heart, and spirit.

Listen to the good. Tune your ears to love, hope, and courage. Tune out gossip and resentment.

Listen to the beautiful. Listen to the music of the masters. Listen to the symphony of nature—the hum of the wind in the treetops, bird songs, thundering surf . . .

Listen critically. Mentally challenge assertions, ideas, and philosophies. Seek the truth with an open mind.

Listen with patience. Do not hurry the other person. Show them the courtesy of listening to what they have to say, no matter how much you may disagree. You may learn something.

Listen with your heart. Practice empathy when you listen. Put yourself in the other person's shoes.

Listen for growth. Be an inquisitive listener. Ask questions. Everyone has something to say which will help you to grow.

Listen creatively. Listen carefully for ideas or the germs of ideas. Listen for hints or clues that may spark creative projects.

Listen to yourself. Listen to your deepest yearnings, your highest aspirations, your noblest impulses. Listen to the better person within you.

Listen with depth. Be still and listen. Listen with the ear of intuition to the inspiration of the Infinite.

Creative Loafing

L EARN TO PRACTICE the art of creative loafing. A survey of creative people indicated that over eighty percent of their ideas came to them while they were away from their desks loafing—walking, listening to music, playing cards, fishing, reading, relaxing in endless ways.

Galileo was finding peace for his soul in a cathedral when he saw a great swinging lamp and conceived the idea of the pendulum. While loafing in the kitchen of his home, Watt noticed the steam lifting the top of the teakettle and from this he developed the concept of the steam engine. Newton was resting under an apple tree when he saw an apple fall and got his idea about gravity. Einstein tells us he was walking in the woods when the theory of relativity first came to him. Darwin remembers the place in the road where the idea of evolution flashed in his mind.

To effectively practice creative loafing, you must learn to constantly keep one eye open for the slightest intimation of an idea. Awareness, sensitivity, and alertness are the keys to producing creative loafing. It is good to maintain an attitude of quiet expectancy, to remember that the supply of ideas in the universe is inexhaustible. I always keep a mental image of an open door in my mind, with the welcome mat out for new ideas. (Don't forget that simple ideas have made many millionaires. Consider the paper clip and the eraser on pencils.)

Loaf with your imagination turned on. See things with your mind as well as your eyes. Have faith that the idea you want will come to you. Do not reject ideas too soon or discriminate against them too severely. Remove all barriers of critical judgement, to provide a free channel for the flow of ideas.

And finally, heed this warning: *Never be without a notebook to record ideas when they flash into your mind. The great idea you forget might have made you rich!*

Creative Love

I HAVE BEEN sitting here in my study going over a book by my friend, Thomas Dreier, published in 1913. He secretly gave this, his first book, to my wife when we were visiting him in Florida in 1950, suggesting she surprise me with it when we got home. It was his last and only copy.

Why I should be going through the pages of this book today I didn't know until I discovered the red pencil marked passage that follows . . . .

"In this book it is especially appropriate to say that the greatest command, the most condensed philosophy, the wisest success-achieving advice ever given was given by a Man who was crucified. He summed it all up when he said, 'Love one another.'

"One does not really need to fight for success. One can love one's way to success.

"Love is more than a gift—it is an investment. It is ready to flow into you, as Emerson says, in a great spiritual stream. Love is a powerful force. Use it. Suggest to yourself that the stream is flowing into you. Then give it out to

others, let your love flow into them. The supply is inexhaustible!"

What Tom says about love is equally true about creativity. Love of people and their needs is the very foundation of ideas. Only ideas that serve truly live. Customers who are loved are loyal. Organizations that radiate love are the only ones that endure. The heart of a true peace is love. Putting love into action is a challenge for creative thinkers. First, love the problem, love the search, love the work. Put your heart as well as your mind into it. Love the cause, the goal. Love the people you serve. Love the product you sell and the people you sell it to. Second, love the 4 creative steps:

✳ *Saturation/Preparation*
✳ *Incubation*
✳ *Illumination*
✳ *Verification*

Move along in the dynamic spirit of love.

Creative Many

"*THE CREATIVE FEW*" is the theme of Herbert Gasson's book, *Creative Thinkers*, which was published in 1930. He wrote: "*In the evolution of the human race upwards, all progress depends upon the production of a comparatively small number of creative individuals.*"

That isn't true today. There is a wave of extraordinary creativity spreading all over the world and more people than ever before are contributing to the progress of the human race. Individuals have unprecedented opportunities to shine forth with innovation and novelty. Everyone can be a creator and share in bringing greater well-being to this planet and its people. For that reason, I dedicate this essay to the "*creative many.*"

Jane Addams recoiled at the possibility of spending her life as a helpless female with no purpose in life.

While touring Europe in 1887, Addams visited Toynbee Hall, the original settlement house in London's East End. Returning home, she purchased the Hull mansion in the slums of Chicago where young women of her station in life could help the poor.

At first, Hull House was simply a first-aid station for the poor. As Addams came to know the poor who were mostly immigrants, more creative programs stressing educational and social services were devised. Millions of Americans owe their success to the influence of settlement houses patterned after Hull House.

Creativity, which invites fresh, dynamic ways of looking at everything is the source of change and newness for people everywhere. It is free to all who will accept it. Creativity does not in any way belong only to the few. It involves an acceptance of the creative power of Spirit and is accessible and available to everyone, though we have scarcely tapped its actual spiritual potentials. True, we are all children of God, but *"it doth not yet appear what we shall be."*

Creativity is not limited to painters, sculptors, composers, poets, and musicians. Wherever life is, creativity can be found. Indeed, there is no spot on this earth where creativity is not needed and where the potential for creativity is not present.

You are creative. You can make a creative contribution to this time in history by giving your support to the good and the true and the beautiful. You can take a new look at your work and make creative changes. You can look at human needs and help supply creative answers.

The magic of creativity touches all things. It works in millions of ways to make a better world. And all these miracles come from God through you, so every individual can make a creative contribution. Together, through creativity, we can discover new ideas, new approaches, new methods, new policies, and a new life.

Creative Meditation

CREATIVE MEDITATION IS being constantly open, aware, and receptive to the goodness of God.

I am out in a boat, fishing on a quiet lake at sunset. I am relaxed and happy. I dream and keep my eyes on the bobber. I go home with a string of perch, and also a string of ideas I caught at the same time.

I go for a walk. I like to walk alone and let my mind drift. I do not push for ideas, but they seem to come with every step. Many of them excite me and I can hardly wait until I can get to my typewriter to set them down.

I read a book with a red pencil in my hand. I'm confident that there are thoughts in the book meant especially for me. They seem to pop out on the page, and when they do I underline them. I always read with great expectations.

I am on a mountaintop. I think climbing a mountain is a great spiritual experience. I gain a new perspective on the world and on my personal problems. I rise above the grim and see the great. I make new resolves to make the most of time. Great ideas for the future reveal themselves.

I am listening to a magnificent symphony orchestra. I'm carried away. I am flying through space among the stars and planets. I am back when knighthood was in flower, riding a white horse, rescuing a maiden. In many ways I become a hero dedicated to saving the world.

I am in bed summing up the day, reviewing my aims and ideals, my plans for tomorrow. I know I'll have the answers I need in the morning.

From a poem, there is this line, which I love: *"Give to the world the best that you have and the best will come back to you."* Creative meditation involves constantly seeking the best, and letting it flow through you into the lives of others, who in turn will be channels to continue the flow of goodness. And lo! We create a new world of expanding love.

Creative Memory

I**T HAS BEEN SAID** that man thinks with his memory. Creatively, man *is* his memory; he is a bundle of impressions built up from an infinite number of sources. The fuller the memory, the greater the creative opportunities.

Stored away in you are all the impressions you have received in your lifetime. Sunsets are there and mountaintops; snatches of poetry, images of art observed, music heard, ideas from the philosophers, prayers, the glory of friendships, spiritual gifts of parent and pastor, the heroes of the great books you have read.

Your memory is a storehouse of thought and experience, and what you have stored away, you can draw upon!

Your memory is constantly growing and expanding, and you can add to the quality of your memories by the thoughts you think, the things you see and hear, the journeys you make, the people you meet, the books you read, and the peak experiences you have. You can consciously enrich your memory day by day. And thus you can widen the horizons of your creativity.

Emerson recorded in his famous journals the observations of a lifetime. He started keeping a journal when he was only seventeen years old and continued for over fifty years, and this proved to be a magic way of aiding his memory. His journals became a gold mine to draw upon for his lectures and essays. It is a plan I too have followed, and recommended.

Another good method is to add to your own memories by tapping the memories of others—by reading biographies and autobiographies of the great men and women who have lived before you.

Great memories make great thinkers!

Creative Miracles

O UT OF A BLOCK of ivory, Pygmalion chiseled the form of a beautiful woman, Galatea. As he worked with inspired zeal a miracle happened. Galatea came to life!

Many potentially happy and successful people are imprisoned in the ivory of defeat and despair. You can help release them to new life through the miracle-working power of your inspiring influence.

When Annie Sullivan became Helen Keller's teacher, she knew that she was able to reach her young pupil before she could instill discipline and a love of learning.

Although she began signing the names of objects into young Helen's hand immediately, it wasn't until Sullivan held Helen's hand under a stream of cool water while spelling out the word "water" that a miracle happened.

As Sullivan watched, Helen became conscious of the mystery of language. Everything has a name and each name gives birth to a new idea.

"One single ray of light", wrote Arnold Bennett, *"one single hint, will clarify and energize the whole mental life of him who receives it."*

Work miracles with praise. Appreciation accelerates accomplishment. People go on to bigger things when they are made to feel that their work is worthwhile.

Work miracles by having faith in others. Thomas Edison was sent home from school because his teacher said he was hopeless. Years later he wrote: *"I won out because my mother never, for a single moment, lost faith in me."*

Work miracles by giving courage. Many ideas have failed to be realized because people lacked the courage to see them through. Promising careers have been abandoned because of fear.

Work miracles by counseling patience. Many a man has turned and left the dock before his ship came in. Stress the wisdom of waiting and working. Time has a great power to solve problems.

Work miracles by expecting great things. People will rise to do the seemingly impossible to justify the high expectations you hold for them.

Work miracles by rousing the imagination. You never can tell what will happen when you set a man's mind on fire with a great dream or purpose. Mentor Graham, Lincoln's teacher, lighted a fire that created the "man for the ages."

Work miracles by setting a good example. *"A boy doesn't have to have a mark on the wall to go by when there is a man around about the size he wants to be."*

Creative Motivation

MANY OF US believe that if we could simply find a quiet, beautiful place in which to think, we would be properly inspired to work miracles! It is a vain hope.

Years ago I read about a writer who was trying to find just such a place. He tried everything. First, he rented an office on one of the upper floors of a skyscraper; but he found himself watching the lights of the city instead of working. Next, he pitched his tent by a stream that ran through a remote area, but spent most of his time fishing and swimming instead of writing. A cabin in the woods did not help either. He was constantly distracted by the activity of the squirrels, birds, chipmunks and other creatures of the woods.

The novel was finally completed on the kitchen table of his home in the city. The moral here is obvious: it is *what* we are, not *where* we are, that counts in creative thinking. The important factors are the depth of our thinking, the impressions we have stored, the breadth of our reading, the experiences and people we have known, our goals and aspirations. Creative power arises from within rather than out of our external surroundings.

I did a lot of kitchen writing myself when I edited and wrote for a number of company magazines in my advertising days. I still recall the reams of copy produced from my notebooks with that old Royal portable. One night I wrote a prose-poem in the lightening fast time of fifteen minutes, inspired by my memory of an old hymn. So far as I know, it is still being read.

Slow Me Down, Lord

Slow me down, Lord.

Ease the pounding of my heart by the quieting of my mind.

Steady my hurried pace with a vision of the eternal reach of time.

Give me, amid the confusions of the day, the calmness of the everlasting hills.

Break the tensions of my nerves and muscles with the soothing music of the singing streams that live in my memory. Help me to know the magical, restoring power of sleep.

Teach me the art of taking minute vacations—of slowing down to look at a flower, to chat with a friend, to pat a dog, to read a few lines from a good book.

Slow me down, Lord, and inspire me to send my roots deep into the soil of life's enduring values that I may grow toward the stars of my greater destiny.

Creative Myth

IN THE WHOLE wide field of mythology, I think the most creative and wonderful myth of all time is that of Santa Claus!

Consider that Santa Claus has put smiles on the faces of untold millions of children, and that he will continue to do so. Has any other myth created so much joy?

Many of the Greek mythological characters were first heroes, and then became gods. Santa Claus started that way too. First of all, he was Saint Nicholas, who lived in the fourth century, A.D. He was bishop of the ancient town of Myra. He was extremely kind and had the reputation of going out at night to deliver gifts. After his death his fame spread all over Europe and now he lives forever in the Santa Claus myth, which has peacefully conquered the world.

Santa Claus reminds us each year of the philosophy of giving. He suggests that gifts should include not only things but also love, joy, kindness, and peace. Emerson's statement comes to mind: *"Rings and jewels are not gifts, but apologies for gifts. The only true gift is a portion of thyself."* (In business there was a time when the Go-Getter was king. Now, the Go-Giver is the true leader, service is his product, and there is a saying that *"he who gives the most deserves the most."*)

As we review history we find that the great givers have always contributed the most to the enriching of the world, and Santa Claus is an inspiring example of the power of giving. He is the world's champion maker of friends and influencer of people.

101

Creative New Year

WHAT MIRACLES WOULD happen if, for just one year, we all resolved to make this a genuinely "Creative New Year."

Manufacturers, looking at their products, would say, *"It isn't good enough!"* and would think about how they could improve it to serve customers better.

Ministers would think about how they could revolutionize their church services to attract and inspire more people.

Husband, wife, and whole families would go into a huddle to discover ways to make their home a different, better, more wonderful place to live.

Would-be authors would forget past rejection slips, dust off their typewriters, and take another crack at writing the great American novel.

Inventors, taking a tip from Edison, who made thousands of experiments in the development of the electric light, would make new attempts to complete their inventions and get them on the market.

Salespeople all over America would begin thinking

about brand new ways that they could present their products to boost sales and demonstrate prosperity.

Educators would begin thinking up ways to improve education, to help students live up to their potential.

Doctors would start expanding their services to consider the needs of the whole patient—body, mind, and spirit.

Politicians would begin thinking about ways that they could serve the people more effectively.

You who are reading this, whatever your work, your goals, your dreams, resolve to put your creative mind to work in the new year. Launch an aggressive, creative drive for new ideas and new ways of doing things, to better serve people. This is your key to a Happy New Year!

Creative Oneness

CENTURIES AGO, a Hindu sage warned mankind of the evil of exclusion. *"Slay the sense of separation which weans you from the rest of the world,"* he wrote.

Ashley Montagu, a modern anthropologist, declared that there is no such thing as race, and that all men spring from common ancestors. *"The existing varieties of mankind are derived from the same ancestral group,"* he pointed out, *"and belong to a single species."*

In living with others on this earth we need to recognize the reality of brotherhood. We are brothers. There are no born bigots. The thought patterns, habits, emotions, and ideals that motivate us are acquired. Biologically we are one, and our task is to create a mental and spiritual oneness. We must stop incorrect thinking before incorrect thinking stops us.

Albert Schweitzer proclaimed a universal ethic that I believe has great power to help us achieve creative oneness. He expressed this ethic in three dynamic words: *Reverence for life.*

When we have reverence for life, we will never do anything to harm, hinder or destroy life. Instead we do everything we can to help life fulfill its highest destiny. We come to realize that when we proclaim war on life, we proclaim war on ourselves, for the same life flows through all of us.

We will not achieve creative oneness in a moment, but it should always be our ultimate goal. Our creative thinking should be concentrated on bringing people together in all those areas that contribute to our common good. We should cooperate instead of fight, believe instead of doubt, save instead of destroy, love instead of hate.

Exclusion builds walls between people. It tears people apart. It separates races, colors, religions, and nations. It divides life. But creative oneness will turn us around. Instead of shaking fists, we will join hands; instead of slamming doors, we will swing them open; instead of building walls, we will tear them down. And instead of rejecting people, we will accept them.

Creative Overcoming

RECENTLY I WAS interviewed about my life as a writer. The first question was: *"What is of most importance in becoming a writer?"* Without hesitation, I answered, *"Overcoming inertia."*

It is true that you'll never write anything until you get down to business and begin writing. However, I do not agree with the usual approach to overcoming inertia . . . will-power, self-discipline, forcing yourself to write.

All the will-power in the world will fail to accomplish anything, unless you have something to write about. Nothing comes from nothing.

Inertia has been defined as *"the tendency of a body to resist acceleration."* You overcome such resistance by the power of your creative thinking. You do not go to your typewriter and sit with fingers on the keys waiting for ideas to come. You go to your typewriter or your yellow pad eagerly, your mind loaded with ideas, plots, themes. Before you can start your typewriter you must start yourself. Once you achieve this mental state you'll not be able to type fast enough to set down all your thoughts. You'll have inertia on the run.

There are several key words that activate creative thinking.

The first is *"Inspiration."* All inspiration is from God but you must seek it. It is everywhere—in crowds and in solitude, in books and speeches, in personal talks with friends and strangers, in children and in the elderly. Think of yourself as a sponge soaking up inspiration. Never let creative ideas escape; hoard them in scrapbooks, notebooks, and in your journal. Expand your thinking to take in the universe.

The second word is *"Enthusiasm."* No one ever wrote a novel until he or she became enthusiastic about the story and the characters began to come alive. As usual Emerson said it all: *"Nothing great was ever accomplished without enthusiasm."*

Another stimulating word is *"Pride."* Proudly visualize your story or article printed in a magazine. Imagine holding your very first published book in your hand.

Inertia is only an enemy when you let it conquer you, and you can put it to flight by the power of your thought.

Creative Parenting

THE ULTIMATE creative act is the birth of another human being, a baby, a child of God . . .

In practicing creative parenthood an ounce of example is worth a ton of preachment.

Your child is watching you *live*, and what you *are* shouts louder than anything you can say.

When you set an example of honesty, your child will be honest.

When you encircle your child with love, your child will be loving.

When you practice tolerance, your child will be tolerant.

When you demonstrate your good sportsmanship, your child will be a good sport.

When you meet life with laughter and a twinkle in your eye, your child will develop a sense of humor.

When you are thankful for life's blessings, your child will be thankful.

When you express friendliness, your child will be friendly.

When you speak words of praise, your child will praise others.

When you confront failure, defeat, and misfortune with a gallant spirit, your child will learn to live bravely.

When your life affirms faith in the enduring values, your child will rise above doubt and skepticism.

When you surround your child with the love and goodness of God, your child will discover life's deeper meaning.

When you set an example of heroic living, your child will measure up.

Don't just stand there pointing your finger to the heights that you want your child to scale. *Start climbing and your child will follow!*

Creative Personality

EMERSON DEFINES THE creative personality when he writes: *"One man pins me to the wall while with another I walk among the stars."*

You know the feeling. Some people seem to lift us up, to inspire us, to bring out our best. Such people multiply creativity; they encourage growth and stimulate progress.

Personally, I owe a great debt to the creative personalities who have touched my life.

One of them was Thomas Dreier. Tom was a business writer I knew for fifty years until his death at ninety-two. His brief statement of his philosophy of writing is something I have lived by, and even if you are not a writer you'll like it because it applies to any kind of creative endeavor. It goes like this: *"As a writer I have only one desire—to fill you with fire, to pour into you the distilled essence of the sun itself. I want every thought, every word, every act of mine to make you feel that you are receiving into your body, into your mind, the sacred spirit that changes clay into men and men into gods—to open doors into a world where you will find the supply of good unlimited."*

And even though Tom is gone now, his influence still lives in me. I turn frequently to his books, many personally autographed to me, to find energy and inspiration for my work. We still walk among the stars together.

Stop now and think of the many who have influenced you.

The point of this little essay is to encourage all who read it to strive themselves to be creative personalities . . . to help others to walk among the stars—to dream dreams, to find themselves, to do good work, to leave their mark.

Here again, perhaps, Tom Dreier shows the way. One day he said to me, *"I have only two simple prayers: God make me loving; God make me useful."*

Creative Plunge

MY KNEES SHAKING, I stood at the very top of the diving tower. Never before had I dared to dive from such a height, though to impress a beautiful young lady I had heroically ascended the ladder. Now, looking down at the water fifty feet below, I was afraid. Would I be a coward and descend the ladder? Would I dive? I hesitated, but finally took the plunge! The young lady was impressed. In fact, a few months later she became my wife. My courage paid off . . . with fifty-eight years of happiness.

Creativity is like that. Taking the "creative plunge" is diving into the depth of life; it is the bold decisive act by which you immerse yourself in problems and challenges. It is attempting so-called "impossibilities." It is a runner breaking the four-minute mile, a swimmer conquering the English Channel; it is mountain climbers reaching the top of Mount Everest. It is you . . . writing a book, building a business, creating an invention, painting a picture, composing a poem. It is you making the most of yourself. You'll never reach your goal hesitating at the top of the tower.

Rollo May, in his inspiring book, *The Courage To Create*, writes: *"Courage is not a virtue or value among other personal values like love or fidelity. It is the foundation that underlies and gives reality to all other virtues and values. Without courage our love pales into dependency. Without courage our fidelity becomes conformism."*

So dive off the tower. Get in the swim. The shock of the cold water will wake you up, get you going. You'll never get anywhere if you climb down from the tower . . . if you insist on staying near the shore. Be courageous! Take the creative plunge!

Creative Plus Factor

THE SPIRITUAL FACTOR can tremendously multiply the power of creative thinking. Let's see how.

The first step in creative thinking is *Saturation or Preparation*. It is a matter of gathering data on the project before you. Now, instead of doing this just by yourself, add the power of prayer. Ask to be directed to certain books and people who can help you. Miracles will often happen. Someone unexpectedly enters your life, the telephone rings bringing you help, you are led to discover a book that can help you . . . or a magazine or newspaper. Pray, and then remain open and receptive.

The second step is *Incubation*, which is turning the problem over to your subconscious mind. Now, think of this as turning the problem over to God instead. The Bible gives this suggestion: *"Wait on the Lord."* Thus, you wait for the doors of the Infinite to open and flash to your mind the ideas you need.

The third step is *Illumination*, in which you depend on your subconscious to inspire you. Now, knowing that you have harnessed spiritual power, you keep your mind in an attitude of prayer. You meditate quietly and confidently, with a high degree of expectancy and awareness. You might, for instance, go for a walk, and as you walk you pray for ideas to be revealed to you. Some of our greatest thinkers use this method.

The fourth and final step is *Verification*. This is a sorting process to select the ideas that are practical and workable. When you apply spiritual power to this step, you ask God to help you with the selection . . . and you evaluate every idea by the standard of the Golden Rule.

The validity of this method is confirmed by the central teachings of Jesus. He said, *"The words that I speak unto you I speak not of myself; but the Father that dwelleth in me, he doeth the works."* And again he said, *"He that believeth on me, the works that I do shall he do also; and greater works than these shall he do . . ."*

There is wide evidence that great men and women in every field of endeavor—poetry, painting, invention, engineering - have achieved their high goals by keeping in tune with the Infinite.

You can, too! Stop trying to do it alone, and make God your partner.

Creative Power

THERE ARE TWO kinds of ideas. First, the idea that you get. Second, *the idea that gets you.*

When I wrote my daughter, who is a novelist, about this approach, she responded immediately: *"The difference between ideas that we get and ideas that get us, is that the ideas we get often fail to inspire us and fill us with enthusiasm. On the other hand, when an idea gets us and we know it is good, it wakes us up and we will go through hell and high water to make it come true."*

The history of ideas that have made our nation great has always been the result of men and women having great ideas take over their lives. So many great ideas grabbed Thomas Edison that he worked night and day to bring them to life. Failure could not stop him. He persisted through 3000 experiments to create a successful electric light bulb. The idea that got Henry Ford was designing an auto the average man could afford. He succeeded, put the nation on wheels, and helped establish an enormous industry. The Wright Brothers were obsessed by the challenge to fly. The great idea that got them was to make a heavier than air craft that could fly and success crowned their efforts.

Amelia Earhart loved to fly. It meant years of discipline and personal sacrifices to learn the vagaries of weather and a man-made flying machine before she could even consider the ultimate challenge—a flight around the world.

What were her thoughts as she taxied her plane down the runway on the first leg of her journey round the world?

Ideas that get people are not confined to material things alone, but to things of the mind and spirit as well. The great ideas of the *Science of Mind* got Ernest Holmes and he developed a spiritual approach that has inspired millions.

The divine idea that got Jesus became one of the Master's chief teachings: *"The Kingdom of God is within you."*

So watch for that great idea and let it *get you.* Surrender to it; give it your all. Energy will flow into you sweeping away inertia. You'll be given the courage to ignore the doubters and skeptics and to get on with your work. Your devotion and dedication will bring victory.

When a great idea grabs you and won't let go you can be sure you have discovered the key to unlimited creative power.

Creative Prayer

M Y WIFE AND I watched a miracle unfold as a beautiful new church was built across the street from our home. It all started when the church organized what they called a "Dream Committee" made up of eight people—four women and four men. In a way this was just another creative thinking group, except that the Great Creator was a member and every session was opened with meditation and prayer.

The purpose of the committee was simply to dream dreams and think up ideas, jot them down and turn them over to the executive committee. The new building came first and other inspirations followed. The committee dreamt with their minds and their hearts and good results were achieved. The church membership doubled, with two crowded services each Sunday. Special community programs were launched. Sunday school grew and was more successful. Dreams became realities!

Everything begins with a creative dream. Far out? Impossible? Perhaps, but as Henry Thoreau said, *"If you build castles in the air, that is where they should be. Now build foundations under them."*

I also like the statement of George Bernard Shaw in his play, *John Bull's Other Island*. He wrote, *"Some men see things as they are and say, 'Why?' I dream things that never were and say, 'Why not?'"*

Praying and dreaming should be a part of all creative thinking.

If the qualities of courage, love, hope, joy, and faith are expressed in your creative sessions, the Great Creator will be working with you.

Creative President

LINCOLN'S DYING MOTHER lovingly drew her weeping boy close to her and whispered the creative command, *"Be somebody, Abe."* His whole life became a creative quest. He read and memorized the poetry of Byron, Bryant, and Whitman. He lived with the Bible and Shakespeare. Tradition has it that he once walked twenty-four miles to borrow a book. His thought was molded by greatness.

In crisis, Lincoln uttered this creative challenge to leadership: *"The dogmas of the quiet past are inadequate to the stormy present. The occasion is piled high with difficulty, and we must rise to the occasion. As our case is new, so we must think anew and act anew. We must disenthrall ourselves, and then we shall save our country."*

To *think anew*, to *act anew*, to *rise to difficulty*—Lincoln used these creative keys to endeavor to unlock and solve the problems of his presidency.

One day, during the War between the States, a committee of Southerners called on President Lincoln.

The leader asked Lincoln if he considered that God was on the side of the Union.

"*Sir*", replied Lincoln, "*my concern is not whether God is on our side. My great concern is to be on God's side.*"

To Lincoln, being on God's side meant expressing the goodness of God—being understanding, tolerant, forgiving, honest, and loving . . . and doing God's will. And it has been said that to live by the faith of Lincoln is to find room for every faith.

Abraham Lincoln—noble spirit, eloquent speaker, master of English, friend of all people, and dedicated American whom I nominate as our most creative President!

Creative Reading

E VERY GREAT CREATIVE thinker is a great reader. He is constantly saturating his mind with great thoughts. He approaches books in this way.

A book lets you set the pace. If you want to stop and think about a word, a sentence or a paragraph the book will stop with you. If you want to close your eyes and meditate about an idea the book gave you, it will be there when you open your eyes, ready to move on with you.

A book synchronizes with your thoughts. It becomes a part of you. The author enters your mind. You can relax and fall asleep over a book and not miss anything, because it does not move until you turn the page. You are in personal control when you read a book, you can accept or reject, agree or disagree and a book won't talk back. A book is your servant.

Books are also a form of immortality. The words

of men whose bodies have long become dust still live in their books. Plato, long dead, is as fresh and alive in his books today, as when he walked the streets of ancient Athens. All the great thoughts that men and women have put into books are instantly available to you. All the great lives that have been lived are told about in books.

A book becomes a part of you, and helps to shape your thinking and your character. The past and the present live in books to guide you into the future.

The spirit of man, the life of man, the discoveries of man, the adventures of man, and the history of man can all be found in books.

Creative Retirement

"*So you are all through, through for good. Now you can sit back and take it easy!*" a friend said to me when I retired back in 1964. That shook me up, for it is exactly what I didn't want to do!

I turned to my dictionary and looked up the word "*retire*." I didn't like what I found: "*Fall back, retreat, withdraw, to remove from active service, to take out of circulation.*" How negative can you be?

So I sought a new word, one that would be full of fire, dash, and inspiration, and I finally came up with "*aspire.*" It is a positive and ongoing word that will fill the future with promise, for aspire means to move forward and seek the best.

With this magic word to guide me, I have experienced a "creative retirement"—writing and publishing eight *Art of Living* books, and for the past 25 years, writing the "Creative Adventure" page for *Science of Mind* magazine.

The very idea of creative retirement reflects a new and desirable approach to the years ahead. Retirement begs for new ideas, different viewpoints, fresh approaches, new faith and hope and love. Creativity can give retirement a completely new and dynamic meaning.

Some time ago I wrote an article for *Modern Maturity* magazine on "The Art of Creative Aging," in which I listed ways of practicing creative retirement: raising roses, serving as lay persons in churches; campaigning for the United Fund; fashioning things with our hands—cabinet work, needlepoint, painting (remember the genius of Grandma Moses?); writing poems, novels, or your autobiography for your family; traveling and making slides for lectures. The possibilities are endless.

There is a great creative idea in this quote from Harry Emerson Fosdick: *"It is magnificent to grow old if only you stay young."*

Meet your retirement with a young mind!

Creative Revolution

EVERY NEW YEAR, the resolution problem comes up. I always know there are hundreds of ways I can improve myself, so I find myself with a big list of resolutions, all of which are broken after a few days of the new year. This year, however, I've decided to go from resolutions to revolution. I'm going to take just one big weakness and give it everything I've got. I'm going to see if I can make one improvement in myself.

In the context of personal development, I like the word *"revolution."* Here are a number of thoughts about it . . .

Revolution is the process of drastic change. In personal revolution, you are your own foe and self-conquest is your goal. It is a bold offensive to change habits, thought patterns, actions, and to establish a new way of life.

It is an about-face. It is turning a corner, taking a new road, moving in a new direction.

It is breaking the bonds of slavery to the past so you can walk in freedom.

It is smashing destructive idols and images and

gaining a new, higher vision of the person you want to become.

It is overcoming the failure complex by beginning to act as though you cannot fail.

It is overcoming fear and making faith your guiding star.

It is a declaration of independence from all that would drag you down, and it is reaching out for all that will lift you up.

Humans alone, of all the creatures of earth, can change their own patterns . . . be their own architects. The philosopher William James declared that the greatest revolution in his generation was the discovery that human beings, by changing the inner attitudes of their minds, can change the outer aspects of their lives.

Let us, then, make this year a year of personal revolution.

Creative Seasoned Citizen

YOU ARE NEVER too old to be a creative thinker. In fact age can be an asset to creative thinking.

I've never liked the term *"senior citizen."* I would much rather be called a *"seasoned citizen,"* one who has been formed and fashioned by all the elements of life: the inspiration of mountaintops, the depth of the sea, the serenity of valleys, the openness of the plains, the majesty of sunsets, the thunder and lightning of storms.

On the stage, neither Helen Hayes nor Jessica Tandy reached the zeniths of their acting careers until they were well past the traditional age of retirement.

Both Carl Sandburg and Frank Lloyd Wright were men who had been so formed and fashioned. Few writers have the scope of Sandburg. He wrote poems and fairy tales for children, two volumes of autobiography, a six-volume biography of Abraham Lincoln— and he topped it all off with a novel. Wright had the vision to start a school for architects, inspiring others to carry on with his methods and ideas. And in his own time he created work places with the radiance of cathedrals. Both men said that they did their best creative work in their seventies and eighties.

For my own inspiration I gathered together a list of other men and women who did outstanding creative thinking in their later years.

While Georgia O'Keefe's career as an artist began when she was a young woman and continued up until the time of her death, primitive artist Grandma Moses didn't pick up her paints and brushes until her family was raised and she was free of daily household chores. Goethe completed *Faust* at eighty, Titian painted masterpieces at ninety-eight. Toscanini conducted at eighty-five, Justice Holmes wrote Supreme Court decisions at ninety, Edison was busy in his laboratory at eighty-four, and Benjamin Franklin helped to frame the American Constitution at eighty. Seasoned citizens carry an aura of victory!

"We do not count a man's years", wrote Emerson, *"until he has nothing else to count."* And an unknown philosopher said, *"There is nothing to do but bury a man when the last of his dreams are dead."*

The contribution of seasoned citizens never dies; everywhere we look are examples of good work to remind us of their creativity.

Creative Seeing

THE EYE IS the camera of the mind. The physical eye sees outside of you, while the inner eye sees within, through your imagination. Consider the many ways those things happen . . .

Emerson said, *"The landscape belongs to you."* And so it does, no matter who owns the land. All nature is yours, through your sense of sight. To deepen the impressions a landscape offers, you can walk down the trail, wade in the stream, swim in the sea, climb the mountain. Through observing body language, you can see human nature. Folded arms often indicate the closed mind: doubled fists are a sign of resistance and fear. On the other hand, open arms usually show acceptance and love, and open fists become the open palms of peace and friendship.

A shy, unattractive young woman married to an outgoing young man with a talent for politics could have wrung her hands and retreated into domesticity when her husband was crippled by polio.

Instead she helped him achieve his political goals. During Franklin D. Roosevelt's four terms as President of the United States, his wife, Eleanor, was his eyes, ears, and legs. Crisscrossing the country and visiting even the most remote areas of the world, she provided her husband with first-hand insights on all she had seen and heard.

Through your eyes you can read books, and the books on your shelves are wonderful guides. With Shakespeare you will discover *"sermons in stones, books in running brooks, and good in everything."* You can encompass the full sweep of life on this planet, as your inner eye is brought into action. You can watch the rise and fall of civilizations, the ebb and flow of mighty battles, and the changing patterns of culture through the ages. When you read biography and autobiography, you can experience thousands of lives in your one life.

Using the faculty of empathy, your inner eye can share victory and defeat, joy and sorrow; you can achieve understanding. From my days in advertising and selling I recall how we used empathy: *"To sell John Smith what John Smith buys, you must see John Smith through John Smith's eyes."*

Through inner vision, see yourself as a happy and successful person. Hold the picture! Then also recognize that inner vision can be extended into the higher realms, through insight, intuition, meditation and prayer!

Genius has been defined as seeing what has been there always, waiting to be seen, and so: *To be more, see more.*

131

Creative Serendipity

K EEP YOUR EYES open, for while you are looking for something else you may discover a treasure. Serendipity may happen to you!

Webster's New International Dictionary gives this definition of serendipity: *"The gift of finding valuable or agreeable things not sought for; a word coined by Walpole in allusion to a tale, 'The Three Princes of Serendip,' who in their travels were always by chance or sagacity finding things they did not seek."*

There are many examples of serendipity at work . . .

"Columbus," wrote Emerson, *"looking for a direct route to Asia, stubbed his toe on America."*

Hoping to express her love, Enheduanna (born ca. 2300 B.C.), the moon priestess and daughter of King Sargon of Agade became the first writer in history, male or female, whose name and work has been preserved.

Pasteur, looking for a way to keep wine from turning sour, by chance discovered the process of pasteurization.

Fleming observed that the blue mold on bread killed all kinds of little bugs. Presto! Penicillin and other antibiotics!

Bell, trying to improve the telegraph, discovered the telephone.

A chemist, trying to duplicate silk fabric, came up with nylon.

While studying the properties of thorium and uranium, Marie Curie instinctively sensed that "something else was present."

After months of work, Curie returned to her lab one evening where she saw for the first time the glow of two previously unknown elements—polonium and radium. She had discovered not only new elements but a new science, and new weapons against disease.

Robert Pim Butchart was a leading manufacturer of cement in Canada. Thirteen miles from Victoria, B.C., a huge limestone quarry was dug. When the limestone was exhausted, the company closed down leaving an ugly open quarry behind. Then serendipity stepped in and inspired the idea of a great sunken garden! This was the beginning of the famous Butchart Gardens, visited by thousands of people each year. The garden covers over twenty-four acres with more than three hundred thousand varieties of growing things, including over five hundred kinds of roses alone!

Serendipity is a magic word for creativity. It demands an open mind and heart and an expectant attitude. Then miracles may be right around the corner!

Creative Simplicity

A T THE END OF a college course in creative thinking, our professor presented each of us a paperback copy of Henry Thoreau's classic, *Walden*, which tells about Thoreau's two-year adventure in a little cabin on the shores of Walden pond. The professor called it "the best book ever written on creativity."

Thoreau was a champion of simplicity. He challenged all of us with the statement: *"Only that day dawns to which we are awake."* And again he wrote: *"Simplicity, simplicity, simplicity! I say let your affairs be as one, two, three and not a hundred or a thousand."*

There came a day when I walked around Walden pond, explored the areas where Thoreau's cabin had been, and collected books about his ideas, including several volumes of his journals. He along with his friend Emerson, have greatly influenced my life.

Simplicity discovered great ideas. Listen to the observation of Charles Kettering, once head of General Motors Research and inventor of the self-starter for automobiles. He said, *"The problem, when solved, will be simple."*

Simplicity uses small words. It practices the wisdom

of Lincoln, who said: *"Make it so simple a child will understand, then no one will misunderstand."*

In one of my books, I wrote, *"The art of simplicity is simply to simplify."* Try to look through the complex and difficult and reduce the problem to simple factors, to everyday matters. You'll find the heart of the problem is basically simple, often obvious.

Simplicity avoids the superficial, penetrates the complex, goes to the heart of the problem, and pinpoints the key factors. Simplicity does not beat around the bush. It does not take winding detours. It follows a straight line to the objective. Simplicity is the shortest distance between two points.

And in these days of high technology, when computers are working their magic, it may be well to consider that mind and spirit are still the greatest factors in creativity. That is the simple truth which yet abides.

Creative Skylight

LONG AGO, Oliver Wendell Holmes wrote of the various levels of thinking. He pointed out that *"there are one-story intellects, two-story intellects, and three-story intellects with skylights."*

The skylight thinkers are those who, in some mystical way, have learned to open themselves to the inflow of Infinite inspiration and power.

We may find it difficult to know where the scientific method ends and the skylight method begins, because the two often work together, but the skylight approach always reaches further and works the miracles.

Leonardo da Vinci, one of the greatest creative thinkers of all time, and a master in many fields, was known to believe in the power of meditating in the dark of night; and he often awakened the following morning with the answers he sought. He also was known to stand for hours before a painting in progress, silent as though waiting for inspiration, and then he would step forward and paint.

Walt Whitman said that when he started a poem, he never had any idea how it would end. He remarked, *"I just let her come until the fountain is dry."* Was some Infinite Power directing his hand?

Haydn, creator of more than one hundred symphonies, said, *"When my work does not advance, I retire into my oratory with my rosary and say an Ave; immediately ideas come to me."*

Gauss, the mathematician, speaking of one of his mathematical discoveries, said, *"At last I succeeded, not by painful effort, but, so to speak, by the grace of God."*

And finally, Emerson well described the essence of skylight thinking. He wrote, *"We lie in the lap of an immense intelligence which makes us organs of its activity and receivers of its truth."*

Creative Solitude

HISTORIAN JAMES TRUSLOW ADAMS made the bold suggestion that we should *"muffle every telephone, stop every motor, and halt all activity someday, to give people a chance to ponder for a few minutes on what it is all about, why they are living and what they really want."*

Until that magic hour comes, each of us must seek out our own moments of solitude for quiet thought and meditation.

Carl Sandburg, poet and biographer of Lincoln speaking before an audience at Princeton, said, *"We need to rediscover ourselves in creative solitude."*

Pablo Picasso, genius of new concepts in painting, explained that for him creation began with contemplation in solitude, that when he contemplated he worked best.

Thomas Edison, who in fifty years of inventing took out over one thousand patents, found that the solitude of his deafness was a creative help and not a handicap. *"I listen from within,"* he said.

Blaise Pascal, mathematician and scientist, observed that *"the miseries of men come from not being able to sit alone in a quiet room."*

Dean Inge defined religion in terms of solitude: *"Religion is what the individual does with his own solitude. If you are never solitary, you are never religious."*

Emerson said that the secret of finding solitude is *"to go to the window and look at the stars."*

Historian, poet, painter, inventor, scientist, theologian, philosopher—all witness to the creative power of solitude.

You can use this creative power in your own life. Strive, not for an isolated, withdrawn solitude, but for an inner serenity and quietness that opens your mind to the inflow of ideas from the infinite source of God's goodness.

Creative Sowers

THE SYMBOL OF the sower scattering seeds is my best image of a creative thinker. Some seeds fall on rocky soil and are lost, while other seeds fall on good soil and last forever.

For more than half a century I have collected good seeds, inspiring seeds, beautiful seeds, and enduring seeds by many creative masters. This makes a treasury of good seeds in two black notebooks of over 500 typed pages.

A few of the good seeds discovered through the years . . .

* A businessman sought to inspire his workers by placing on each desk a card which read: *"You can do it!"* The result was unexpected. One young man eloped with the boss' daughter!
* One hundred years after his death, Ralph Waldo Emerson is still the most quoted inspiration writer in the world. His good seeds runneth over!
* This quote will surprise you—*"Books on how to succeed are read by very few successful men."*

❋ This from Eleanor Roosevelt—*In the long run, we shape our lives and we shape ourselves."*
❋ *"These are not books . . . but minds alive on the shelves."*—Gilbert Highet
❋ *"The only possible metaphor one may conceive of for the life of the mind is the sensation of being alive."*—Hannah Arendt

I have found keeping these notebooks through the long years a rich adventure with creative sowers. I recommend it.

And then there is the thrill of creatively sowing ideas and inspiration into the minds of others. Often our contributions will actually change lives by sharing appreciation, courage, love, and joy.

Carry the ideal of being a creative sower, that you are on the side of growth, plenty, peace, and progress. Make it a point to scatter creative seeds every day of your life!

141

Creative Spears

I N ALL THE millions of words written by Shakespeare, I have discovered three quotations which I call, "*The Three Spears of Shakespeare.*" I call them that because they are sharp and get to the point, and I think they especially apply to anyone who aspires to become a creative thinker. (If you wish to look up these three spears in the writings of Shakespeare, the first will be found in *Julius Caesar*; the second and the third are from *Hamlet*.)

The first Spear: "*The fault, dear Brutus, is not in our stars, but in ourselves, that we are underlings.*"

For us as creative thinkers, success depends not so much on outside influences as it does on inside attitudes and resolves. Our destiny is not in the stars but in our own hands. We may not have the power to change the world but we can change ourselves. We must apply initiative and imagination.

The second Spear: "*There are more things in heaven and earth, Horatio, Than are dreamt of in your philosophy.*"

This suggests that the creative thinker should never be satisfied, but should continue to explore all dimensions of life. He will not seek one exclusive point of view, but all points of view. The spirit of the creative thinker is limitless; there are no boundaries. He is constantly aware and alert. He is research in action. He knows that perpetual growth is the key to genius.

The third Spear: *"This above all: to thine own self be true, And it must follow, as the night the day, Thou canst not then be false to any man."*

To be true to ourselves certainly means that we must be true to our deepest insights, our noblest impulses, and our highest ideals. It means that our creative thinking will be built on a foundation of character. Emerson said it well in one sentence: *"Nothing is at last sacred but the integrity of our own mind."*

Creative Spirit

OUR MINDS ARE unconquerable if we have a spirit that never surrenders to defeat. Spirit is everything! It is the spur, the energizer, the dynamic that turns defeat into victory.

Many years ago I read a stimulating little book entitled, *The Creed of the Conquering Chief*, which has disappeared from my library but which I always remember. The basic thought of the book is the fact that we are all *"minute builders,"* which means that, to get the most out of life, we must inject spirit into every minute.

I was inspired, too, by a discovery made by Dorothea Brande. For twenty years she was a mediocre writer. She had a few short stories published, but the novel she started was never finished. Then, upon reading a book on psychology, she learned that there is a *Will to Fail*, as well as a *Will to Succeed*. She realized that many of us dodge the real labor of thinking and do everything we can to avoid making an effort, telling ourselves that if we tried we could set the world on fire . . . but we never try. So Brande came up with a maxim that changed her life: *"Act as though you cannot fail."* It lifted her spirit and worked miracles. In just two years she wrote three books, two of which became best-sellers, and she outlined three more novels, as well as giving dozens of lectures around the country.

Spirit sustains us through ups and downs, failure and success. It is the power that keeps us going. If we have spirit, we'll never quit. We see spirit working in sporting events, when pure determination will frequently carry an inferior team to victory. Spirit is enthusiasm, dedication, devotion, faith, hope, energy, and vision.

Spirit is the unbeatable quality that assures ultimate success. A creative spirit equips us to channel infinite power. Creative spirit transforms ideas and dreams into realities!

145

Creative Stance

J UST AS THE stance is important in Golf, the right creative stance is important in Life.

As you face the challenge of a new day here are some of the factors in a good creative stance . . . .

You begin by keeping your head UP. You face the day unafraid. You believe in yourself and your cause and stay as alert as a champion golfer teeing up for a tournament.

You take a firm grip on positive attitudes of thought. You hold right thoughts in your mind just as your hand grips a golf club. You keep both feet on the ground. You stand for the highest and the best and strive to fill your life with the goodness of God.

You think straight. You endeavor to correct slices and hooks that may cause you to wind up in the "roughs" of life. You guard against mental traps. You eliminate the kinks in your thinking. You take a good, clear realistic view of the situation before you tee off for the day.

You keep your eye on your goal. Just as you try to make each stroke contribute to a great game of golf, you strive to make each day add up to a great life.

You assume a victorious attitude. Just as the golfer visualizes the ball dropping into the cup, you see yourself closing the sale, giving an eloquent speech, creating a great idea, baking a perfect pie . . .

Don't just plunge into your day. Pause and get set.

Take the creative stance.

Creative Supply

Do you remember the words: *"It takes a heap o'livin' in a house t' make it home . . . ?"* It was in one of Edgar Guest's most famous poems—and he wrote thousands of them. Guest started as a reporter for the Detroit Free Press but soon turned to poetry. He didn't call it poetry, but said, *"It could be verse."*

A poem a day was his goal and he kept that rate of production up for over fifty years. His poems were soon in syndication in hundreds of newspapers around the world. Guest not only wrote poems, but he also recited them well from memory, and was a popular speaker.

After Guest had died, I was at a meeting where his son was speaking. He told me about one time when his father came home from the office. He seemed discouraged and downhearted, which was very unusual. He asked that the family gather around together for dinner because he had bad news for them. Dinner was usually an up-beat time, with stories and laughter, but this night it was dull and somber. Something was terribly wrong.

After dinner Edgar spoke. He said he hated to tell his family but the fact was that he was finally "written out." There would be no more poems. He was afraid he was finished as a writer. He hoped the family could adjust to the situation and carry on. His wife and children left the table in despair, not knowing what to say or do. Dad had never been like this before.

The son went on with the story, saying that attempts to encourage his father got him nowhere. Finally the son went upstairs to his room almost in tears. He tried to read and listen to the radio but nothing would help. At last, discouraged and depressed, he went to bed.

At midnight he awoke; he had been aroused from sleep by a familiar sound, the clickety-click of his father's typewriter. Another idea had come and Dad couldn't wait to begin writing again!

The lesson here? Never give up as a creative thinker! Ideas are inexhaustible. When you open yourself to them, they will come to you, and you can never use them up.

Creative Surprise

Back in January 1964 when my first article appeared in *Science of Mind* magazine I selected "The Creative Adventure" as the name for my page. Creativity is in itself a philosophy of life. It looks for the best. It seeks improvement. It represents people at the very highest level of thought and life. It attains union with the Creative Force we call God.

I got to thinking of creativity in the family and found myself writing the following words:

"Everybody enjoys a happy surprise."

A surprise brightens dull days and awakens people to the glories of life. Surprise is a creative word. It suggests doing something new, unexpected, different, or dramatic.

Bring home a bouquet of roses for your spouse. Whip up a loved one's favorite dish. Take the kids to the circus. Go camping. Attend the fair. Throw a party. Write a letter to a long-neglected friend. Phone someone long distance. Get out of the rut. Make people happy. Surprise them!

Put the element of surprise into your work. Generals win battles by surprising the enemy. Through your imagination you can change your actions, your habits, and your plans. Come up with something original. Blaze new trails. Surprise your customers, clients, or patients with new services and ideas!

Surprise yourself. Discover your unique talents and possibilities.

Explore new hobbies. Paint a picture. Write a poem. Break away from old routines. Get up early and add an hour to the fresh end of the day. Walk more instead of always driving. Read something entirely different from what you have been reading. Break the shackles of inertia and get that long-neglected project under way. Surprise yourself and you'll be surprised at the fun you'll have.

Creative Teaching

ONE OF THE MOST inspiring examples of the creative influence of a teacher is found in the biography of Mentor Graham. From the moment he met the boy Abe, Graham became aware of Lincoln's potential. All of Graham's resources as a teacher, all that he knew, all that he himself had learned, *everything*, was concentrated on one goal—to help Lincoln to grow and make something of himself. Graham gave him books to read, he taught him grammar, he disciplined him and awakened him to his possibilities. And Lincoln responded.

And one proud day Mentor Graham was present in Washington to see his pupil inaugurated President of the United States of America. What a victory in creativity!

Mentor Graham lived into his eighties, teaching almost to the very last. His body is now buried in New Salem, Illinois and on his tombstone are the words, *"Teacher of Lincoln."*

And Graham's creative influence lives on in the life of Lincoln because more books have been written about Lincoln than have been written about any other American. And today Lincoln's own writings have been published in two volumes, including all of his speeches, letters, and presidential papers.

Has any other teacher ever had such a great pupil?

All teachers are capable of creating responsible young men and women who go forth to live good lives. The influence of the creative teacher touches about everything. Every nook and corner of human activity calls for creative people. We look to teachers to supply those people. Creative teaching is one of our greatest needs.

Creative Thanksgiving

You are made in the image of God. You are only a little lower than the angels. You are a co-creator with the Creator. Pause then at this thanksgiving season and give thanks for the miracle of selfhood.

Give thanks for yourself, for your health and strength and energy. Ponder the miracle of your body, which, without your conscious thought, controls heartbeat and respiration, digests food, compounds chemicals, renews cells, combats disease, heals wounds, and maintains equilibrium among its huge and intricate array of separate parts.

Give thanks for your power to think. You stand at the doorway of your mind and select the thoughts that make you what you are; you create yourself. Give thanks for your creativity and the ideas that come to you and inspire you to serve others.

Give thanks for your immortal spirit, which you can keep ever open and receptive to the eternal flow of the goodness of God.

Give thanks for those who have labored through the ages to create the world you live in today. Acknowledge that you are the heir to the infinite riches of all the great original thinkers of the past.

Be thankful for all those who have helped you to grow—your teachers, parents, employers, friends, spiritual guides, and others, acknowledging them by name. Be thankful for the good books which you have read, inspiring sermons and talks you have heard, as well as your own notebooks and journals.

Finally, be thankful for the challenge of your own personal future. Be thankful for your dreams, your ideals, your hopes. There are unlimited possibilities ahead.

Creative Thank You

"*THANK YOU*" is a beautiful phrase, whether spoken or written. Using it is a good way to scatter the seeds of love and goodwill.

Make the Postal Service your partner in sending "thank you" messages all the days of the year. I wrote a minister in praise of a sermon. It arrived on one of his "low days" and gave him a lift. Perfect timing.

For all the precious gifts of the Spirit—a song, an orchestra, a dramatic performance, a great novel—show your appreciation with a "thank you."

For the parents who raised you, taught you, and showed you the way, keep saying over and over again, "Thank you so much."

For your spouse who worked beside you and supported your dreams, for your lovely daughter, your thoughtful son, your wonderful grandchildren, write often to say, "Thank you for being you."

For teachers, scouting leaders, and mentors who not only inspired your desires, but also supported your endeavors.

For those friends far away, whom you never intend to forget, surprise them with letters saying, "Thanks for the memories."

Now and then in newspapers, magazines, and books you will find things that you wish to share: cartoons, jokes, wise sayings, poems, news items. Clip or copy and send them on to someone who will likely respond to you with a "thank you."

Photographs are often the next best thing to a visit. Tuck them in with your letters. They personalize your "thank you."

Be creative and plan your own way of saying "thank you." Thank God for the magic words "thank you." The more they are used, the happier our world will be.

Creative Thinker

FOR MANY YEARS I have had, here on my desk, a replica of Rodin's masterpiece, *The Thinker*. Often I sit and gaze at it and meditate about what it implies.

To me it is man making his greatest discovery, the power of thought. I am reminded of these beautiful words: "*Cosmic consciousness slept in matter, dreamed in the animal, and awakened in man.*" This is what is happening in Rodin's inspiring statue. It is man wrestling himself free from the physical. It is the kingdom of the mind beginning to unfold. It is the emergence of selfhood. It is God coming into man's awareness.

The Thinker is symbolic of man's waking up to his infinite potential. It suggests that there are no barriers, that the mind is limitless and inexhaustible, that it is a reflection of the Divine. It warns us to struggle constantly against the gravitational pull of matter. It challenges us to break away and rise on the wings of thought, for it is through the mind we reach toward the stars; through the mind we contact the Infinite.

It is the mind that sets us free to make our dreams come true. There are no mental jails or prisons when we use the key of creative thought.

Anaxagoras, an early Greek philosopher, wrote: *"All things were in chaos when Mind arose and made order."* The Thinker seems to say: *"Make way for mind. Mind is unconquerable. Unshackle it from selfishness, fear, and defeatism. Have faith in the ability to do the impossible. Mind is the miracle worker!"*

My suggestion to you is to secure a replica of The Thinker to inspire you. I don't know where they are to be found, but they are around somewhere and worth a search.

Creative Unthink

HUMANTICS, AN ORGANIZATION in Wynnewood, Pennsylvania had been sending out a motto which is just the opposite of the *"Think"* motto we have seen so often. This time the word is *"Unthink."* In small type under the word this statement is made: *"Thinking causes trouble. Unthink stops trouble."*

Creativity, as we all know, is far more than conscious thinking alone. Often we can be more creative by coasting in a free-wheeling manner, permitting the power of Infinite Intelligence within us to work things out.

I'm reminded of a line in Annie Payson Call's fine book, *Power Through Repose*. She wrote, *"If we are free and quiet, the poem, the music will carry us and we will be surprised at our own expression."*

One day, while walking through the gardens at Bok Singing Tower, near Lake Wales, Florida, I came upon a plaque with a message on it for me, from John Burroughs. *"I come here to find myself,"* it read. *"It is so easy to get lost in the world."*

I followed the advice given. I thought it was high time I found myself again. I sat on a bench, and surrounded by beauty, tried to stop all thinking. I let my mind wander. I closed my eyes and listened to the song of the birds.

Suddenly the chimes in the tower were playing my favorite hymn: *"Oh God, Our Help in Ages Past, Our Hope for Years to Come."*

To grow as a creative thinker you, too, need time to Unthink.

Creative Visualization

I HAVE READ AND HEARD about many approaches to using the creative power of visualization, but one is outstanding, in my opinion. This method was invented and developed by my friend, the late Harold Sherman, a well-known metaphysical writer and speaker.

At his retreats, Harold came onstage, sat in a chair, and then asked us to relax with him as he himself relaxed. We were to release tension from our shoulders, our neck—out to our fingertips, down to our toes. *"Let go of yourself,"* he would say. *"Become like old rag dolls."*

Next he would ask us to close our eyes and visualize a movie screen, our very own personal movie screen. From here on he would ask us to play the role of movie director and movie star. We were to see ourselves on the screen, successfully doing whatever we wanted to do—giving a speech, making a sale, being interviewed. We could see ourselves winning an award or being praised by our boss. On the physical side we could see ourselves walking vigorously, playing golf, or even making a hole in one. In everything, we saw ourselves as positive and constructive.

We could also bring to life on our mental movie

screen great men or women whom we admire. We imagined their voices telling us secrets of success and happiness. We memorized quotes from their writings and speeches and repeated the words to ourselves as we visualized the people speaking. It would be as though they appeared in person before us and advised us.

Mental movies are limited only by our imagination. They can take us around the world—to a mountaintop or to a quiet lake. We can run off reels of happy memories, of times gone by. We can see ourselves graduating from college or loafing in a hammock. The mental pictures we create are our own private way of bringing a better, happier, and more joyous future into being.

Mental movies—visualizations—will make deep impressions on our subconscious mind and help to bring us the success and happiness we desire.

Creative Walking

WHILE WALKING ACROSS the Golden Gate Bridge on a bright and sunny day, I was reminded again of what a dynamic force walking is in stimulating creative thinking.

Back in my advertising days we believed that there was creative magic in taking a walk. If ideas wouldn't come as we sat at our desks, we practiced what we called, "The Hat Trick". We donned our hats and went for a walk. It almost always worked.

Many great thinkers were great walkers. Einstein is said to have found walks around the Princeton campus helpful in working on his revolutionary ideas about time and relativity. Freud is said to have done much of his thinking, and his teaching as well, while walking. Emerson, who faithfully wrote in his Journal every day, captured ideas while walking, then rushed home and wrote them down. They became the basis for his lectures and his essays. One of the most creative ad men I know tells me he gets his best ideas on the two miles of sidewalk between his home and his office.

Men have been walking and thinking for centuries. In the sixteenth century, the humanist philosopher Erasmus counseled his followers, *"Before supper walk a little; after supper do the same."* Perhaps what thinkers need to do today is to get off wheels and get back on their feet!

I think walking might be considered meditation in motion. Walking wakes up the cells and glands, stimulates the heart, expands the lungs, and makes us fit to think—so the flow of ideas often quickens with every step. And it is good to carry a notebook to jot down the high points of your thinking at such times.

If you have been trying unsuccessfully to develop ideas from your desk, your easy chair, or your bed, try *meditation in motion* for a change. Take a walk.

Creative Work

WORK IS THE FINAL, vital step in creativity. Work is expression. It is the mind in action. Religions, philosophies, formulas, projects, programs, plans, ideas, and ideals are inert until work infuses them with power. The greatest truths of God and the mightiest ideas of man remain static and unfruitful until we work to make them live.

Work releases truth, so it can inspire and regenerate; work releases ideas so they can bless and benefit. Without work nothing happens.

Rejected by governmental and medical authorities, Clara Barton continued to carry medical supplies and cared for the soldiers wounded in the American Civil War until she was finally appointed superintendent of nurses for the Army of the James.

Barton returned to the battlegrounds during the Franco-Russian War where she took part in the work of the International Red Cross. In 1881, Barton helped establish the American Red Cross, not only for military personnel, but also for civilians threatened by calamities, famines, natural disasters and epidemics.

Your own dreams, hopes, aims, purposes, and ideas mark time until you start them marching. Work is the magic that creates miracles.

What kind of work? Work that is dedicated and devoted; work that never gives up; work that can meet defeat after defeat and bounce back; work that keeps on keeping on; victorious work!

Carved in the heavy oaken door of the Roycroft Inn, in East Aurora, New York, are these immortal words of Elbert Hubbard: *"The love you liberate in your work is the love you keep."*

To do great work one must fall in love with work. Cellini, the goldsmith, pouring his whole soul into his creations, made masterpieces, and the love he thus liberated brought him the praise of kings. I've seen the designer of a piece of machinery pat it with pride as he might pat the head of a son. It was a part of him. He had built his personality into it. He loved it. Luther Burbank loved his work with flowers and other plants, and he thrilled the world with his new creations. Henry Irving, working for more than thirteen years to perfect his acting of Macbeth, a part he loved, found his love coming back to him in the applause of his audience.

Work is the key to achievement, and when it is done in the spirit of love it glows with a mystic quality no one can explain. And as workers we feel as did Robert Louis Stevenson, who wrote, *"I know what happiness is, for I have done good work."*

Creative Zest

IN OUR APPROACH to creative living, we must widen our usual vision, for creativity is not limited just to thinking. It goes far beyond thought, and includes the *total self.*

Everything we are gets into the act when we create. Creativity includes many factors—our health and energy, our emotions, our visions, and our love and devotion. At best, creativity involves our full power, focused on what we have a burning desire to achieve.

In my search for a one-word definition that would take in all of these factors, the best word I could find was *"zest."* The dictionary defines it this way: *"Spiritual enjoyment, wholehearted interest, gusto."*

I especially like the phrase, *"spiritual enjoyment,"* since, as a rule, we take being creative too seriously. We struggle and strain when we should be relaxing and enjoying the process. We should approach creativity as we would fun and games. Thus we open ourselves joyously to the flow of ideas. We put ourselves in tune with the Infinite.

It is great to experience creative zest. It gives us a sense of wonder and curiosity about the universe and about people and events. It gives us the boundless energy to explore, adventure, and experiment with new ideas. It inspires us to make our lives count by giving ourselves to worthy causes and projects.

Zest goes beyond dreams. It uncovers ideas and then makes them realities. It carries through and gets the job done. Zest also urges us to strive for the best, to set ambitious goals, to reach for the stars.

All of this suggests a new dimension of creativity in which the thinker's personality, knowledge, and experience are all applied to problem-solving. It suggests a dynamic, daring, victorious approach that can transform the process by which we give birth to newness.

CREDO OF A CREATIVE THINKER

I BELIEVE THAT THE creativity that twisted a piece of wire into a paper clip and put erasers on pencils is great enough to create brotherhood and universal peace.

I sow the seeds of creativity by the height, depth, and breadth of my daily living. Great books are my Bibles. Great men and women are my heroes. People are always under my mental microscope.

Creativity flows from Infinite Intelligence, through me. And through me has the power to work miracles.

My role is to remain ever open and receptive to the Creative Spirit; to be quiet and still and eternally aware of the magnificent flashes that may light up my mind. I believe that the highest thoughts, the most noble ideals, the greatest ideas may come into my world through me. The doorway of my mind is always swung wide open to invite creative power.

My creative creed is to cooperate with all creative thinkers that we may band together to enlarge the scope of creative living for all people.

My creative aim is to serve as a creative channel to help make freedom ring around the world.

I dedicate myself to growing as a creative thinker—experimenting, testing, studying, meditating, and praying—so that I may make a creative contribution to my time and to the future.

SUGGESTED READING

Creativity has been a lifetime hobby. Through the years I have collected every book on creative thinking that I could put my hands on. Finally I gave this entire collection to Michigan State University.

Most of the titles listed here may be available to you in your library. Some may still be in print in your regular book store or may be found in book stores specializing in out-of-print books. A good out-of-print house that has been successful in finding books for me many times is:

Chicago Book Mart
P.O. Box 636B
Chicago Heights, IL 60411

Applied Imagination by Alex Osborne
The Art of Clear Thinking by Rudolph Flesch
The Art of Practical Thinking by Richard Weel
The Art of Thinking by Ernest Dimnet
The Art of Thinking by D.D. Runes
The Art of Thought by Graham Wallas
Awakened Imagination by Neville Goddard
Building Your Idea Power by Nations Business

Cogitators Treasury by Sam Goodman
The Courage to Create by Rollo May
Creative Mind by C. Spearman
Creative Mind and Success by Ernest S. Holmes
Creative Power by Gred H. Giswald
The Creative Power of Mind by Willis Kinnear
Creative Power of the Mind by C. Larson
The Creative Process by B. Ghiselin
Creative Thinkers by Herbert Casson
Creative Thinking Charles Whiting
Creativity and Its Cultivation by Harold H. Anderson, Ed.
Dynamic Thought by Henry Hamblin
Executive Thinking and Action by Frederick De Armond
The Future of the Human Mind by Gross and Estabrooks
How to Create New Ideas by Jack W. Taylor
How to Develop Your Thinking Ability by Kenneth Keyes
How to Develop Profitable Ideas by Otto Reiss
How to Get Original Ideas by Edward Wortley
How to Keep Mentally Fit by Lowell Thomas
How to Think Creatively by Eliot Hutchinson
How to Think Up by Alex Osborn
How to Use Your Head by William Reilly
Ideas Have Consequences by Richard Weaver
Idea Tracking by Frank A. Armstrong
The Knack of Using Your Subconscious Mind by J.K. Williams
The Law of Intelligent Action by William Reilly
Let Me Think by H. A. Overstreet
The Magic of Thinking Big by David J. Schwartz

174

The Mind in Action by Eric Berne
The Mind of the Maker by Dorothy Sayers
The Miracle of Mind Power by Dan Custer
More Power to Your Mind by G. Milton Smith
Our Free Minds by H.A. Overstreet
The Practical Cogitator by Curtis & Greenslet
The Private Papers of Henry Ryecroft by George Gissing
Productive Thinking by Max Wertheimer
The Sources of Invention by Jewkes, Sawers and Stillerman
The Subconscious in Business by Robert Updegraff
The Techniques of Creative Thinking by Robert Crawford
Think For Yourself by R.P. Crawford
Thinking in Business by Herbert Casson
Wake Up Your Mind by Alex Osborn
Your Creative Power by Alex Osborn
Your Mind and How to Use It by W.J. Ennever
Your Subconscious Power by Charles Simmons

ABOUT THE AUTHOR

Born at the turn of the century, Wilferd A. Peterson, has been writing all of his life. He cut his teeth editing and publishing company magazines for Jaqua Advertising Agency, while also working on his own writings. In 1961 the editor of *This Week Magazine* (a national Sunday Supplement) thrust Bill into fame by publishing his inspirational messages. Every week 14 million people read his writings, and thousands wrote urging him to author a book.

Working with Henry Simon, editor at Simon and Schuster, Bill published his first book, *The Art of Living*, at the age of sixty. Since then, he has written book after book, with over a million copies sold. For the last twenty-five years, he has written a monthly column for *Science of Mind* magazine, and once again, his readers have urged him to compile these essays into a book for easy reference. *The Art of Creative Thinking* is Bill Peterson's response to those many requests. In these busy times, readers are sure to appreciate his economy of words, which express significant insights which can be grasped in only a few minutes.

At ninety, Bill Peterson is still growing, and showing his readers how they can continue to expand their horizons in creative ways.

If you would like to receive a catalog of Hay House products, or information about future workshops, lectures, and events sponsored by the Louise L. Hay Educational Institute, please detach and mail this questionnaire.

We hope you receive value from *The Art of Creative Thinking*. Please help us evaluate our distribution program by filling out this brief questionnaire. Upon receipt of this postcard, your catalog will be sent promptly.

NAME _____

ADDRESS _____

_____

I purchased this book from:

☐ Store _____

    City _____

☐ Other (Catalog, Lecture, Workshop)

    Specify _____

Occupation _____ Age _____

We hope you receive value from *The Art of Creative Thinking*. Please help us evaluate our distribution program by filling out this brief questionnaire. Upon receipt of this postcard, your catalog will be sent promptly.

NAME _____

ADDRESS _____

_____

I purchased this book from:

☐ Store _____

    City _____

☐ Other (Catalog, Lecture, Workshop)

    Specify _____

Occupation _____ Age _____